HAUNTED
NORTHUMBERLAND

Winter's Gibbet near the village of Elsdon. A harrowing reminder of times gone by.

HAUNTED
NORTHUMBERLAND

Darren W. Ritson

*This book is dedicated to the North East Ghost Research Team,
members past and present (2003-2011)*

First published 2011

The History Press
The Mill, Brimscombe Port
Stroud, Gloucestershire, GL5 2QG
www.thehistorypress.co.uk

© Darren W. Ritson, 2011

The right of Darren W. Ritson to be identified as the Author
of this work has been asserted in accordance with the
Copyrights, Designs and Patents Act 1988.

British Library Cataloguing in Publication Data.
A catalogue record for this book is available from the British Library.

ISBN 978 0 7524 5861 8
Typesetting and origination by The History Press
Printed in Malta.

Contents

Acknowledgements

I would like to thank fellow researcher and author Mike Hallowell for his tireless support and help, and for writing the foreword to this book. To my family and my close friends who have shown unyielding support during my many years of adventures. To everyone that I have spoken to and have been involved with during the research process of this book I give you my most sincere thanks. Special thanks must go to John Triplow for the help and assistance he has given me, including certain texts and images used herein; to Suzanne Hitchinson for sharing her thoughts with me regarding certain locations within this book and for supplying me with additional photographs to reproduce herein; to photographer and paranormal investigator Gail Ward for her kindness and allowing me the use of two of her images; and to Mark Winter for accompanying me on many of my endeavours – cheers pal! I must also thank the Newcastle Library and Information Service for the use of some of the other images produced herein.

All photographs taken by Darren W. Ritson unless otherwise stated.

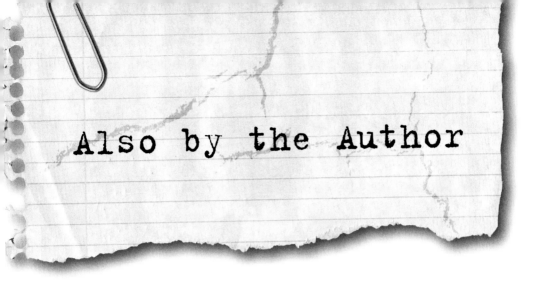

Also by the Author

Ghosts at Christmas
Haunted Berwick
Haunted Durham
Haunted Newcastle
The Haunting of Willington Mill: The Truth Behind England's Most Enigmatic Ghost Story
(with Michael J. Hallowell)
The South Shields Poltergeist: One Family's Fight against an Invisible Intruder
(with Michael J. Hallowell)

Foreword

I first met Darren W. Ritson many years ago when we both joined a local paranormal investigation group. Darren was still 'cutting his teeth' in the ghost hunting world back then, but I recall being bowled over by his enthusiasm and eagerness to help.

Please don't think that I'm implying that Darren was a novice in paranormal research at this juncture: he wasn't. Although I hadn't had the privilege of working with him previously, it soon became obvious that he was an expert in his craft – and I don't use the term 'expert' lightly. As I was to discover, he had a huge archive of ghost-related material stored safely within the confines of his cerebrum.

Later, Darren and I would develop a working partnership and write several books together. Working with him on these projects has been one of the highlights of my career. The down-side is that I'm riven with jealousy, as this book on the ghosts and spectres of Northumberland is one which I'd truly liked to have penned myself. Still, his knowledge of Northumberland ghosts is more comprehensive than mine, and so he has done a better job than I could have done. Sometimes my jealousy overcomes

me, though, and I still get the urge to poke him in the eye with a big sharp stick.

Seriously though, it's sad to say, but the world of paranormal research is rife with rivalry and factionalism. Darren has been subjected to this – as have I – in no small measure. Critics doubted that he'd ever have one book published, let alone several. He ignored their *ad hominem* attacks and went on to pen some of the best works on the subject I've ever read. Not only has he confounded his detractors, but he's also delivered to posterity a record of some of our region's most enigmatic hauntings. For this he should be commended.

There are two kinds of people in this world; those who believe in ghosts and are fascinated by them, and those who don't believe in them and aren't interested at all.

That old wit Samuel Johnson once observed, 'Nothing concentrates a man's mind more wonderfully than the sure knowledge that he is to be hanged in the morning'. To paraphrase the diarist, I'd also add that nothing will turn a sceptic into a believer more quickly than seeing the ghost of the hanged man that very afternoon.

There has been a trend recently to make the whole enterprise of ghost hunting

A line drawing of Chillingham Castle – said to be the most haunted castle in Britain.

more technical. Investigators often burden themselves with a myriad of gadgets and gizmos, all of which – allegedly – will chip away at the defences of a wraith or phantasm and enable us mere mortals to establish once and for all their existence. There's nothing wrong with this as such, but we need to be careful. Ghost hunting from a scientific perspective is laudable, but we don't want to end up jettisoning the romance and wonder of it all. There is a mystery surrounding apparitions; an eeriness and otherworldly ambiance which enchants the ghost hunter like nothing else can do. When I hunt ghosts I like to soak up the 'atmos' and revel in it. I rejoice in mental images of foggy Victorian streets, ominously silent castles and windswept moors – all of which are perfect settings in which to see a spectre. I'd hate to kick into touch all that romance, or sacrifice the atmosphere surrounding hauntings on the altar of scientific advancement. To me,

ghosts without a spooky ambiance are like empty whisky bottles – of no use at all.

Some time ago, Darren and I were being interviewed by someone from the BBC and we were asked, 'What is your most memorable experience?' It took Darren and I a while to answer, for there are many we have to choose from. Ghost hunting, if it's engaged in properly, can provide the investigator with a lifetime of memories to look back upon in old age.

Ghost hunting is not something that you can teach someone. True, you can give the rookie investigator all the tools of the trade and allow them to benefit from your years of experience, but in the final analysis it has to be said that a good ghost hunter relies primarily on instinct. You have to have a nose for a good story, a gut feeling which enables you to separate the true encounter from the misunderstanding and the real paranormal experience from the hoax. To be honest, you either have it or you don't, and Darren certainly has it. Like the coyote hunting its prey, a good ghost hunter will follow wherever his or her nose takes them.

One of the good things about ghost hunting is that it helps immensely to preserve our folk history. Literally thousands of strange experiences have been documented by dedicated researchers like Darren, enriching our folklore to an incalculable degree. The UK is fortunate to have produced a long line of investigators, each of whom have cottoned on to an enigma or mystery and immortalised it in print for the edification and entertainment of others. Entertainment? Yes! I make no bones about the fact that reading a good ghost story – factual as opposed to fictional – is an incredibly pleasurable experience. If anyone tells you otherwise, they're fibbing.

I remember sitting with Darren in the home of Guy Lyon Playfair, one of the elder statesmen in the world of paranormal research. We were drinking Earl Grey tea and eating biscuits. Guy popped out of the room for something, and, almost in hallowed tones, Darren whispered, 'Can you believe we are actually doing this?'

I knew exactly what he meant. Guy has spent decades researching the unexplained, and sitting in his study – crammed with books on the most arcane subjects – was, to us, akin to sitting in the fabled Library of Alexandria. Those who write about ghosts are inheriting a mantle that has been passed down for generations. Researchers like the late Harry Price, Peter Underwood, Guy Playfair, Colin Wilson and the late Maurice Gross are links in a long literary chain which connects us to the wonder of the world we live in, and both Darren and I have been privileged to meet and interact with many of these men. As the author of several excellent books on ghost hunting, Darren has now became yet another link in

that metaphorical chain and industriously goes about his business of informing his readers that there truly is more to this world than Horatio could ever dream about.

In 2007, Darren and I spent a night at the infamously haunted Chillingham Castle. We'd been invited to attend by the editor of *Vision* – a magazine we wrote for – to take part in a ghost hunt, interview celebrity medium David Wells, and write up the experience for readers. We saw no ghosts of armoured knights, no headless horsemen or phantasms of medieval serving girls (more's the pity) but neither of us were surprised. Ghosts rarely appear to more than one witness at a time, and since the castle was filled with dozens of amateur investigators from all over the UK we knew our chances of having a real paranormal experience were 'Slim to none, and Slim was out of town', as the Americans say. Still, it was all in a good cause.

The truth is that ghost hunting – real ghost hunting, that is – is nothing like the way it's portrayed on television. Spirits do not leap out from every darkened corner, and terrifying groans do not rent the air asunder with monotonous regularity. In the vast majority of cases, nothing happens at all. That's why real ghost hunters, like Darren, need to be tenacious; the biggest enemy of the paranormal researcher is – and should be – boredom. If you're seeing spooks every five minutes and are convinced that the face of Winston Churchill can be seen in a photograph of an 'orb', then you need to calm down and ask yourself whether ghost hunting is really for you. If you really want to see strangeness in the mundane, then carry on; but real investigators do not. They want to witness that much rarer phenomenon – strangeness set apart from the mundane.

Perhaps I should explain. Our world is filled with things that we do not understand. That doesn't make them paranormal; it just makes them currently inexplicable. Look around you and you'll see thousands of inexplicable things. It's a free country, and if you want to believe that these things are paranormal then no one has a right to stop you; but you'll be missing out on a lot. Hidden amongst the myriad of pictures of 'orbs', the 'supernatural' noises made by an antiquated heating system and the 'cold spots' caused by a stiff northerly wind blowing in through an ill-fitting window frame – all of which you can delude yourself are 'paranormal events' – there are the rare occurrences which are well and truly breathtaking. True sightings of ghosts are light years ahead of anything a fertile imagination can dream up. They leave one with a sense of wonder, a feeling – almost impossible to adequately articulate – that one has experienced a glimpse of another reality. When you've really seen a ghost, you won't be left wondering about the veracity of your experience – you'll know.

Ghost hunters enjoy the thrill of the chase, and it's that very factor of uncertainty that sustains us as we go about our admittedly weird business. It's because we don't know whether the Grey Lady of Chillingham Castle really exists that we keep going back there in the hope that, maybe one day, we'll find out for ourselves. The chances may be brutally slim, but that doesn't deter us. Like I say, we revel in the thrill of the chase, not necessarily the end result.

From left to right: Mark Winter, the author, celebrity medium David Wells and Mike Hallowell at Chillingham Castle. The author and Mike Hallowell had interviewed David Wells for **Vision** *Magazine and were about to take part in the charity investigation that was to be held there.*

Thomas, Earl of Lancaster, is reputed to haunt the ruins of Dunstanburgh Castle. Does he? I do not know, but that hasn't stopped Darren researching the story and writing it up in this book for you, the reader, to wonder at. In one sense it doesn't really matter, for this superlative Northumberland legend has taken on a life of its own. It has become a living, breathing thing; a vignette in our folklore that enriches our past, present and future. We would be the less for not having the legend, regardless of whether or not we ever see the ghost.

I must confess that Darren has the advantage of me in one respect. He revels in ghost tales that have a great deal of romance attached to them. I'm a bit of a Philistine when it comes to ghost hunting, and whilst Darren is looking for the spectres of fallen soldiers on the battlefield of Flodden, I'll probably be looking for one in a tenement flat in Sunderland. Whereas Darren yearns for an encounter with the shade of a sixteenth-century Northumbrian Earl, I'll likely settle for the spectre of a chap who used to run the bookies on the High Street. I'm too old to change now, and I'm set in my ways. That's why I probably couldn't write a book like this. Darren is still a young strip of a lad compared to me, and has set his sights a bit higher. Good for him, I say. He'll deliver you a much better class of ghost.

Darren W. Ritson is one of the world's most dedicated ghost hunters. Through hard work, a detail for accuracy which Borders on the obsessive and a gut instinct honed to perfection, he has drawn together dozens of tales from our region which will prove to be a delight to all who read them. *Haunted Northumberland* is a veritable treasure trove of the mysterious, the enigmatic and the downright eerie. If your life is too calm and your mind too settled, then this book will cure you. You may become unnerved after the first few pages and, by the last, engulfed in the very essence of dark paranoia – but it will have been money well spent!

Haunted Northumberland is a shining example of everything a good guide to ghosts should be. Being honoured with writing the foreword to it is something I'll never forget.

Read on, enjoy, and be terrified, my friend …

Michael J. Hallowell, 2011

Introduction

NORTHUMBERLAND is without doubt an exquisite region of mystery, intrigue, romance, enchantment and great aesthetic beauty. It has had a very turbulent history due to the many years of warring with our Scottish neighbours, resulting in it being steeped in eerie folkloric fables, miraculous myths and legends of long ago. So it has been an honour and a privilege to have been given the chance to pen this work. I have long wanted to include a book on Northumberland in my forever growing number of literary works and now, thanks to hard work and tenacity, another of my dreams has been realised. Did you know that Northumberland has more castles – ruined as some may be – than most, if not all of the other counties in the UK? The 'land' that is 'north' of the River 'Humber' (North Humber Land – although nowadays the Borders between the counties have changed even though its name remains) is home to over forty-five bastions and strongholds, and the best part of them are reputed to be haunted.

That is almost forty-five tales of ghosts before we even begin. Some of the castles are said to house more than one ghost, so that bumps up the total yet again! Then we have pubs, inns, hotels, B&Bs, parks, beaches, stately homes, churches, battlefields to consider too... The list is endless, which is why I've decided to pen this work.

Don't think for one second that I have nailed down just about every shade, denizen, phantom, spook, spectre or ghost that Northumberland has to offer: on the contrary, for I have barely scratched the surface. There are literally hundreds upon hundreds of ghosts allegedly roaming Northumbria. In fact, there are so many its a wonder we don't see them on a daily basis – or do we? Many accounts come in of people from all over the region – and beyond – and from all walks of life, all bearing witness to strange Northumbrian phenomena. I, for one, am fascinated by these stories. I am lucky enough to have been the recipient of many of these reports, and many emails and letters arrive at my home describing these ghostly encounters. Some of these have been included herein and are published for the very first time.

To me, Northumberland – as daft as it may sound – is the 'South West of the North'; let me explain. Counties like Cornwall, Devon, Dorset, Somerset and

Alnwick Castle; one of the many magnificent inhabited bastions that adorn Northumberland. A superb example of a Northumbrian stronghold.

Wiltshire *et al* have long been associated with magical tales of ghosts and wraiths that roam the land forever, in search of a resting place. Some folk suggest that the land in which this area of Great Britain is located has certain properties within it that enhance the paranormal activity that takes place here. With places such as St Michael's Mount, Tintagel Castle, Avebury Stone Circle and Stonehenge, one may be inclined to agree that this notion may have some actual truth behind it. Ghost hunters from across the globe

travel to the UK to visit the shores and inlands of these mystical places and as far back as I can remember, the south west of England was always known as, or at least considered by the experts to be, the UK's paranormal capital. Northumberland, in my eyes, is just as mystical – if not more so – than anywhere in the south west. It must be stressed that in addition to what you are about to read about in these pages, mysterious man-beasts and big cats are also thought to roam the Northumbrian lands. Sea monsters and other giant-fauna

Norham Castle near Berwick-upon-Tweed, one of the many magnificent, albeit ruined, fortresses that litter Northumberland.

An old map of Northumbria (c. 1400) by Robert Morden. (Courtesy of Newcastle Libraries and Information Service)

types are said to lurk in the cold and rough North Seas just off its rugged and romantic coastline. UFOs festoon the Northumbrian skies like enigmatic fireflies and kelpies, braggarts, sprites, fairies, bogles, brags, barguest and redcaps are all thought to await you around almost every corner you choose to turn, but that, my dear reader, is another book entirely …

This particular book has been stocked to the gills with tales of ghosts that Northumberland has to offer – and by Jove there are many to tell. In fact, the amount of tales I came across during my travels and

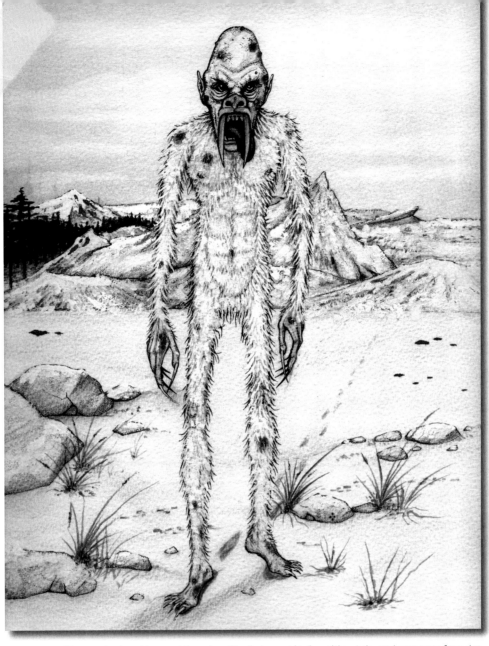

Ghosts and poltergeists are not the only entities that are said to 'haunt' the windswept barren terra-firma that is known as Northumberland. (Courtesy of Graham Hallowell / Thunderbird Craft and Media)

research for this book number into their hundreds, and there is a distinct possibility I could pen another book just on the ghosts alone; who knows, one day I may do just that. The reader will notice that I have not mentioned Northumberland's fabulous history too much either, because quite frankly it has been told a million times over already. This is a ghost book, not a history book. However, due to the fact that ghosts are linked with historical events I have included small snippets of relevant historical information that accompany certain sections contained herein, but just enough

*The rolling hills of Northumberland;
such a beautiful, yet mysterious place.
(Courtesy of Suzanne Hitchinson)*

to familiarise the reader with the 'haunted locale' that we are dealing with at the time of reading. Northumberland has indeed a rich and varied history, and most turbulent too, so if the reader wishes to read up and learn more about Northumberland's historical past, then might I suggest they check out the recommended reading section at the back of this book.

If I may, I will now say that Northumberland truly is a magical place to visit, so if you don't come from there, or have never been there, then I suggest you pack up your bags and book yourself into one of the many wonderful hotels, inns, hostels or caravan sites that festoon this ancient landscape and go and spend some time there. If you are an active ghost hunter (or indeed, merely someone with a passing interest in ghostlore), and are in much need of scary thrills, then Northumberland is most definitely for you. I can not recommend it enough. Finally, I hope you, the reader, will enjoy my creepy collection of Northumbrian ghost tales as much as I have enjoyed researching them and writing them up. Remember, if you do visit, or indeed if you actually reside in this wonderful part of the UK, keep your eyes peeled and your ears to the ground because you just don't know when it will be your turn to run into one of the many denizens of the Northumbrian otherworld that have roamed this ancient land over the last 2,000 years or so.

Darren W. Ritson, 2011

An A-Z of the Ghosts of Northumberland

Apparitions on the A1

I often begin writing books of this nature with the sentence, 'Where better to begin our ghost tour of (place name) than right here at …', but this time I won't. Don't want things to become a bit repetitive. I will begin, however, by saying that I remember not so long ago hearing the amazing tale of a ghost that had saved the life of a driver who had crashed his car. It is a tale of great mystery and intrigue. The story begins after a young European lady had been dropped off by a motorist. It is thought that she was holidaying in Scotland and had decided to hitch a lift down into Northumberland. By all accounts she was 'dropped off' somewhere along the side of this busy road between the Border town Berwick-upon-Tweed and the town of Morpeth. This dropping off led to a tragic accident, as she was subsequently run over and killed by a speeding car.

Exactly one year later, a doctor and his companion were said to have been driving home late at night when the car headlights lit up a hiking woman who was standing at the roadside. She was described as having fairish hair, and she was wearing a raincoat and holding a backpack. They pulled over, as it was a cold and foggy night, and asked if she needed any assistance. She uttered no words, but as she stood there, shaking, she pointed towards a copse of trees at the foot of an embankment. Hidden away in the trees, and barely visible, the doctor and his companion noticed a wrecked car. The doctor decided that the woman was fine, but in shock, and rushed to the car wreckage; his companion drove away immediately to find a telephone in order to raise some help.

The doctor found a man in the front seat of the car who had suffered serious injuries to the head; he was still alive and so the doctor stayed with him and administered first aid until the ambulance finally arrived on the scene. His intervention had helped keep the man alive. Once the ambulance had taken away the injured man the doctor turned his attention to the woman – but he not could find her. After asking the medical staff and the others who were now on the scene if they had seen the woman – they replied that they had not – he was left dumbfounded. Where could she have gone? After the man had been taken to hospital – and when he was well enough

An artist's impression of the phantom hitchhiker that was seen on the A1 motorway somewhere between the Border town of Berwick-upon-Tweed and the town of Morpeth. (Courtesy of Julie Olley)

Pinpointing the exact location on this long and busy stretch of motorway was a difficult task, but I managed to more or less nail it. Bearing in mind that the A1 today is one of the busiest – and one of the most dangerous – roads in the country, I have decided to omit the whereabouts of the 'drop off', the tragic accident and, of course, the actual ghost sighting. I don't want to be held responsible for any more accidents or deaths in this area. One ghost at this location is enough, don't you think?

to speak – he was interviewed. According to the reports, he claimed he was driving alone in the dark when, suddenly, a woman wandered out onto the road directly in front of him. He attempted to swerve out of the way but it was too late and he hit her. As he made contact he was sickened to feel her 'crunch' as she went under the car. He then careered off the road, down the embankment, and crashed into the copse of trees.

Going back to the European woman who was run down and killed in this area. Records show that her description matched exactly with the doctor's description of the mystery woman who had appeared at the scene of the accident on that night; fair hair, raincoat, carrying a travel bag or backpack. Make of this what you will, but it leads me, and others, to think that the woman that the doctor and his companion had seen by the roadside was the ghost of the unfortunate traveller who had been killed there exactly one year earlier.

The Hooded Monk of Alwinton

Alwinton is located about 20 miles west of Alnwick and lies at the top of the Coquet Valley on the outskirts of Northumberland National Park. The Hooded Monk of Alwinton is a rather well-known ghost that is attached to this area, so what self respecting Northumbrian ghost hunter would omit it while compiling a gazetteer of Northumberland's finest ghost stories … not me, that's for sure! There is, however, not that much to the tale, to be honest, but what is known is well worth retelling in these pages. The ghost – or at least its sightings – are said to date back to the 1960s, when a number of people reported seeing a monk-like figure drifting around a lonely spot up near the moor area.

Something that makes this story a little different from the other ghost stories or monk stories is that this particular spectre is seen with no face, no hands and no feet and is said to hover above the ground. It is as though nothing but 'floating robes' frequent the area. According to Peter Underwood in his book, *The A-Z of British Ghosts*, the haunting was investigated by the Newcastle Institute of Psychical Research in 1967. Sadly the society does not exist anymore, so efforts to find out what they may or may not have uncovered during their investigation proved fruitless. I would indeed like to know more about this cowed phantom, however, so if anyone knows anything – or if you were once part of the Newcastle Institute of Psychical Research – then please do contact me and tell me all about it.

An artist's impression of the phantom monk of Alwinton. Its lack of face, hands and feet make this spectre a truly terrifying one; go in search of it i f you dare! (Courtesy of Drew Bartley)

Bamburgh Castle, Bamburgh

Lying around 20 miles south of Berwick-upon-Tweed, and approximately 40 miles north of Newcastle-upon-Tyne, is one of the north of England's most notable historic strongholds, Bamburgh Castle. Nestling high on basalt crags, yet in the same respect almost on beach level, Bamburgh Castle most certainly dominates the area in which it is situated. With the most spectacular views and panoramas being enjoyed by those that visit, there are many reasons why one could pay Bamburgh Castle a visit.

The Norman keep which remains intact on the site of Bamburgh Castle was probably built by Henry II, while excavation has shown the site to have been occupied since the first century BC. The castle played a very large and a most crucial role in the infamous War of the Roses in 1464, and – by all accounts – was the first castle ever to succumb to cannon fire in the UK. The imposing and elevated keep is the oldest remaining part of the castle and can be seen from miles away on clear days. Most of the bastion was destroyed during bloody sieges and wars but the magnificent keep remains miraculously unscathed, retaining its original stonework. In the eighteenth and nineteenth centuries, much needed restoration began on the castle.

In 1894 it fell into the hands of the Armstrong family after the first Lord Armstrong saw it and decided to immediately purchase it. Its restoration subsequently – and thankfully – continued, and today the castle stands proud as a reminder of those turbulent bygone days. For me personally, it is the symbol of the rugged Northumbrian coastline.

There are, to my knowledge, two ghosts associated with Bamburgh Castle, with the first being that of a knight in full shining

armour. This phantom has reputedly been seen and heard in the great Norman keep as he rattles and clatters his way through the dark chambers at the foot of this ancient edifice. As for the other ghost story … well, there seems to be varying accounts of just what, or who, this second ghost really is. The first version of the ghost lady of Bamburgh was relayed to me during my early school days. I had been staying at a centre for schools at nearby Seahouses during a week's holiday away with my class. During the course of the week we ventured along to Bamburgh Castle, where our teachers told us about the 'Pink Lady'. We were informed that this elusive phantom haunted the castle battlements and surrounding sand dunes.

The 'Pink Lady', we were told, was thought to have been a Northumbrian princess who once resided in the castle. She fell in love with a man who was subsequently sent overseas by her father simply because he did not believe in their relationship. This broke the princess' heart, and she vowed to wait for his return. Thinking the princess would soon give up on waiting for her love, her father left her to her own devices. Eventually, after waiting many years with no sign of her lover, her father decided it was time for some devious action. In an effort to put her off, he invented a story about how the man in question had somehow contacted him and explained that he had met another woman on his travels and would not be coming back for his daughter. This ploy backfired on him in the most horrendous way. After hearing the dreadful news, she took herself to the top of castle (while wearing her favourite pink gown, as the tale goes) and hurled herself to her death on the jagged rocks below. We were told that her ghost is seen every other year standing in the sand dunes with her pink gown blowing in the North-Sea breeze as she waits hopelessly for her long, most certainly lost love.

This ghost account has featured in a number of ghost books I have seen over the years, and perhaps this is where my teachers learned about it. Indeed, I have recently featured it in my own book, *Supernatural North*. But since then I have discovered another ghost at the castle: a phantom lady, this time known as 'Green Jane'. She is a ghost that is said to been seen near a gate close to 'the green' inside the castle grounds. Dressed in a cloak, this hooded woman has been observed holding on to a small bundle wrapped in a cloth. As she begins to walk towards the green, she is thought to stumble and fall over. As she falls over she is said to 'cry out in alarm' before falling down a flight of stairs and out of view. Those that rush to her aid find no woman at the foot of the stairs but often hear a chilling laughter coming from …well, nowhere, it seems.

The woman was thought to be a young beggar called Jane. It is said that she was sent to the castle by her poor family in search of food and other provisions that would have been useful to her impoverished family. Upon approaching the postern gate, she was accosted by castle guards who teased her and made fun of her poor condition. As they pushed her away, she is thought to have tripped and fallen down a flight of stairs to her death. The bundle that her ghost has been seen carrying around turned out to be her baby. She had taken the infant with her

The magnificent keep at Bamburgh – haunted by a knight in armour that can been seen, but is more often heard, clattering his way through the undercroft.

in a vain attempt to get the sympathy vote from those at the castle. The baby was said to have died in the fall too.

One wonders if the two ghosts (the Pink Lady, and the Green Lady) are one and the same. Although the stories have some big differences, they have their similarities too: the Green Lady falls to the ground, just as the Pink Lady fell from the top of the castle. They are both very distraught and lost individuals, and they both (some folk think) wear a garment that gives them their respective 'ghost names'. Over years of telling, ghost tales quite often suffer from 'Chinese

An artist's impression of the ghostly knight in armour that is seen in the undercroft of the great keep at Bamburgh Castle. (Courtesy of Julie Olley)

whisper syndrome' and become rather distorted, to say the very least. Having said that, it may just be possible that there is no mix up at all and that two ghost women haunt the magnificent Bamburgh Castle. I guess its for you, the reader, to decide.

Bay Horse, Stamfordham

In the Northumbrian village of Stamfordham, between Newcastle and Hexham, is the Bay Horse pub. This one-time fortified farmhouse dates back to 1590 and was originally a coaching inn. The Bay Horse is a wonderful locale with an awe-inspiring ambience, which certainly does give it an air of mystery, or overt mystique. It is one of two pubs that sits in the centre of the small hamlet from which visitors can enjoy amazing scenery of the Northumbrian countryside.

The Bay Horse pub has a ghost or two, and apparitions have been seen here many times over the years by different people and at different times. There are reports of phantom footfalls being heard on one of the inner stairwells, anomalous lights have been recorded on their CCTV, and poltergeist-like upheaval has been reported in certain areas. It has even been suggested that a tunnel lies below the pub, adding further to the legends which adhere to this mysterious old inn.

I know of a number of individuals who have had the pleasure of spending a night at the Bay Horse inn looking for signs of its alleged paranormal activity although sadly, the author has not yet had the privilege. The team that has investigated the pub claim to have had an interesting night, during which their medium 'picked up' on many things, including a spectral priest in the pool-room area; this presence was verified by the owners of the inn. Although the rather unscientific and subjective method of rod and crystal dowsing was employed by the team, they claim other spirits managed to communicate with them. Of course these results must be taken with a pinch of salt. However, other devices which were used, such as EMF meters and night-vision video cameras, add a little credibility to the overall results of the investigation.

With both sound and light anomalies being recorded, the night was deemed as 'interesting' by their team leader, who came to the conclusion that multiple entities seemed to reside in one of the bedrooms. Whether the results of this overnight investigation are to be taken seriously or not is down to the reader, but the fact remains for many years now this wonderful old-Northumbrian pub has had the reputation of being haunted.

The Bay Horse public house in Stamfordham. Haunted by apparitions and other strange paranormal phenomena; it is a well-known haunted inn of Northumberland.

Berwick Castle

Nothing much remains of the one-time fortress that was Berwick Castle. The castle, which sat in probably the most ideal position in which a castle could sit, was once the home to many different Scottish and English Kings. The railway station at Berwick now occupies most of the castle's former site, with the platforms being located where the magnificent great hall would have once been situated. Upon arriving at Berwick-upon-Tweed by train – as I have done on many occasions – you can see the gaunt remains of Berwick's old castle as it slopes down the rather steep embankment towards the river – it is a sight

to behold. As the train pulls into the station, it is rather hard to get your head around the fact that where you now sit was, at one time, a full-working, and much-attacked bastion. Its rather sad to think that Berwick Castle is now long gone, never to be seen again. However, if you know where to look, you can see buildings and stone constructions that have been actually made from the stones of the old fortress, namely the Royal Border Bridge, and the Berwick Barracks.

The Prince of the Cumbrians, the twelfth-century ruler otherwise known as King David I, built the castle during his reign, 1124 – 1153. Later, it was to be re-built and modified by Edward I (Longshanks) following Berwick's great siege of 1296.

The walls grew to an impressive 50ft in height, and being almost 12ft thick you would think the bastion would indeed be impenetrable – but it wasn't. The castle, over its long history, was captured and recaptured many times, despite that fact it was standing on a natural rock outcrop and overlooking the Tweed. The edifice dominated the whole area, and thus it was one of the best strategically situated castles in the land, and yet it was besieged and taken on thirteen occasions. Between 1296 and 1482, the township of Berwick was subjected to what we call the Great Border Wars between the English and the Scots, and it is these battles and fights between the two countries that now give Northumberland its wonderful, but bloody, history. When the Border Wars came to an end, the castle was nigh on inhabitable; it was decided that it would not be rebuilt. It subsequently fell into a state of disrepair, and all that remains today is a stretch of wall known as 'the white wall'. This leads from the train station area and down to the river, and guards and ominous flight of steps known locally as 'Breakneck Stairs'.

There is only one ghost that is said to reside on the site of the old castle, and it is that of a Scottish piper. It is said that he can

The ruins of Berwick Castle as they slope down the embankment towards the River Tweed.

An artist's impression of the phantom piper that has been seen on the ruined walls of Berwick Castle. (Courtesy of Julie Olley)

Native American 'whoops' and 'wails' of the battle-cry as they advanced on horseback – the drone of the bagpipes made the enemy nervous.

The last sighting of the infamous ghost piper of Berwick Castle was, I was told, back in the early 1970s. A train passenger, who was travelling through Berwick on his way back home to Edinburgh, spotted him. Ascertaining more details regarding this sighting proved rather tricky, to say the least, so verification was rather difficult. Was it the story being re-told to keep the legend alive? Or did a bona-fide sighting take place of the ghostly piper? Until the next sighting is reported (or the sounds of mysterious pipes being heard in the vicinity are reported), I guess we can only speculate as to whether or not this ghost is real. I, for one, think its a wonderful story and would love to think it is an authentic one.

Bellister Castle

Bellister Castle, in Haltwhistle, dates from around the thirteenth century, with its ghost dating from the sixteenth century – or so it is said. Not much remains of this one-time fortified house, with the crumbling ruins standing on a small hillock behind a copse of trees, just off the A69. This grade II listed building, which was built by John De Blenkinsopp in around 1480, is now in the hands of the National Trust after many years of occupation, significant rebuilding and many alterations.

With many of its original buildings now lost in the sands of time, the castle still has a significant presence due to its position on the hill. Bellister is also believed to have its own ghost too – that is why, of course, it is featured in this book.

be seen, but is more often heard, as he paces back and forth along the old castle walls, playing his bagpipes. He has been seen on the wall leading down to the river, and is also believed to haunt the section of castle wall that stands at the very foot of the steep embankment, close to the river and by the now-modern pathway. In the days of the Border Wars, the bagpipes were employed by the Scots to instil fear and dread into the advancing English armies. The sound of the pipes was a sound that no English man had heard before; it was similar to the

The legend of the 'Grey Man' dates back to a murder that once took place hundreds of years ago. It is said that the [then] Lord of Bellister came across a minstrel that was trespassing on his property and subsequently, and with no remorse, set his pack of vicious hunting dogs upon him. The dogs raced towards the terrified man, growling and snarling as they approached him. Then they sunk their razor-sharp teeth into the unfortunate man's neck, torso, arms and legs, and tore at his defenceless body. They ultimately killed him, by savagely ripping the poor chap asunder. The minstrel is said to wander the grounds and castle of Bellister Hall forever, trying to come to terms with his untimely and unnecessary death.

It has been said that visitors to the grounds and ruined castle have also heard the sound of growling dogs coming from near to where they are situated. Usually, after nervously looking round for a dog or for something that may account for the 'growling' noise, nothing is found. I recently spoke to one individual who claimed to have had this very experience back in the late 1990s. After spending half an hour or so looking around and taking some photographs, she decided to take a stroll up the road that runs towards the private living quarters of the establishment. When she got half way up, she heard a frightening snarling noise coming from directly behind her. She stopped dead, froze, and then slowly turned round, expecting to see a Doberman, or perhaps a Rottweiller – she saw nothing. She was adamant that whatever she heard was directly behind her, and upon turning round to see it, she told me that 'the

Bellister Castle in Haltwhistle is haunted by a ghost known as the 'Grey Man'. (Courtesy of Newcastle Libraries and Information Service)

Blenkinsopp Castle (c.1890) The ghost here is known as the 'White Lady' and dates back 600 years. (Courtesy of Newcastle Libraries and Information Service)

snarling ceased'. She knew nothing of the legends attached to Bellister Castle, and she has never been back since. I spent an afternoon at Bellister a few years ago hoping to catch of glimpse of the Grey Man, or even hear for myself the sounds of the Lord's baying hounds – no such luck!

Blenkinsopp Castle, Northumberland

Blenkinsopp Castle is a ruined old shell that is part fire-damaged and part demolished. A nineteenth-century mansion house stands next to this one-time fortified home, which originally dates from the fourteenth century. It has been classed as a scheduled ancient monument, and is recorded as a grade I listed building.

The manor of Blenkinsopp was held by the Blenkinsopp family in the thirteenth century, but they vacated the property in the 1500s, and left to live at Bellister Castle. The Earl of Northumberland then took Blenkinsopp over. By the early 1830s, the castle was disused and was left abandoned for many years, until William Blenkinsopp Coulson carried out major restoration work on the building, bringing it back to its original state. Shortly after the renovations, however, they sold the building on and moved away. In the twentieth century the buildings served as a grand hotel, until fire destroyed the building in the mid-1950s. Due to this tragic inferno, parts of the castle were demolished, on the grounds that the structure was deemed as 'unsafe'.

The ghost of Blenkinsopp Castle is known as the 'White Lady', and dates back 600 years. Bryan De Blenkinsopp is said to have married a woman so rich that it took twelve strong men to carry her gold to the castle. Bryan was a greedy man by all accounts, and he was livid that his wife had ordered the servants to bury her treasure and gold in the castle – so he could not get his hands upon it. After much searching for this 'hidden gold', and after many refusals from his wife to tell him where it was, he decided to leave Blenkinsopp Castle and tell no one about his whereabouts.

For over a year, his grief-stricken wife screamed and shrieked the place down, wondering where her beloved had gone. She blamed herself for her husband's disappearance and thought how things would have been different if she had shared her gold with him. She sent out her servants to scour the coutryside for any sight or sound of her husband, but each and every time they returned without him. She eventually went out looking for him herself. This ended in disaster too, as it is said that she never returned. Both Bryan De Blenkinsopp and his heart-broken wife were never seen again.

It is said that Blenkinsopp's wife, tortured by remorse and ridden with guilt, can not – or will not – rest in peace. Her ghost is said to wander the castle until her treasure is discovered and her beloved returns. Perhaps, when this is done, she may finally rest. This ghost is also said to haunt Thirlwall Castle too. An underground tunnel was said to have been found that links both castles together, and it is in this tunnel where the White Lady has reputedly been seen – at each end. More on Thirlwall Castle later in the book …

Buffalo Centre, Blyth

The Buffalo Centre, in the Cowpen area of Blyth, is now a community centre. However, in days gone by it was a thriving meeting place for locals, in the guise of a much frequented alehouse. The pub was named the Buffalo Inn, and the building dates back to around 1841. *Pigots' Trade Directory* for 1834, however, lists an inn or a tavern on Keelman's Row called The Red Bull. It is possible that this is the original Buffalo Inn building.

I had heard rumours through a friend of mine, Cindy Nunn, that the building was suffering from 'paranormal activity', and I was asked if I would like to venture up to investigate the claims. Cindy and her associates had spent some time in the premises seeking scientific data to support the claim that the building was haunted. She told me that she had had a rather satisfactory night of investigating and recommended that I should pay a visit.

I agreed to do this, but first I wanted to speak to young lady, and her friend, who lived in the apartment on the top level of the building. It was these people who first brought the alleged haunting to Cindy's attention. As Cindy wanted a second opinion from me, on the results she had gathered, I made efforts to contact the tenants. It must be stressed that she told me absolutely nothing about anything she may, or may not, have experienced during her overnight surveillance there. This is the right way to go, of course, because if I could could come up with with similar reports on my stay there, it could go some way as to proving the case, so to speak.

On interviewing the occupants of the flat, I discovered that a rumour

The Buffalo Centre in Blyth; this one-time pub is haunted by two ghosts.

persisted of an alleged hanging believed to have taken place in the building many years ago. No records exist to verify this statement, but that's not to say it never occurred. It is, however, rather unlikely. I also discovered that nothing of an allegedly paranormal nature had occurred in the actual flat. The ghostly phenomena that was being reported came from downstairs and inside the centre. I was told that the sound of chairs being moved around, their metal feet being scraped across the wooden floors, was quite often heard by those living in the flat above. This scared them somewhat, as they knew nobody was inside the centre. At the time, the building was well and truly locked-up from within and 'no one alive' (their words) was inside the property. I was also told that doors were often heard to slam closed, and footsteps, echoing over the wooden floors, were heard coming from down below. Again the building was locked up for the night, and no one was left in the building – bar the girls in the flat. During my chat I was also informed about two actual ghosts, or apparitions, that had been seen inside the centre. The first was described as 'an old man in a black coat', who was reported to have been observed standing by the fire-exit doors on the lower section of the premises. The other 'figure' was alleged to have been seen standing in the hallway. The girls had no idea who these figures could be.

On my visit I brought along a mediumistic friend of mine called Glenn. During the course of my interviews with the flat tenants, I had insisted (as did Glenn) that he should sit in the office well out of earshot. This was, of course, to prevent Glenn from hearing about any ghostly accounts or learning of any odd occurrences before he was to carry out a reading. It's interesting, to me personally, to see what so called mediums pick up on, as I like to put them to the test too. I knew Glenn had no knowledge of the venue, or its ghostly goings on, so it was fascinating to see what he picked up. The first thing he told me during the reading was that there had been two ghosts, or figures, seen in the property. He then went on to identify where they had been seen. Glenn mentioned the moving chairs, the footsteps that had been heard, and many other incidences that were verified by both the tenants and Cindy. How he did this I do not know: either he is an extremely good guesser, or he may really be psychic.

Later on, while investigating the workshop area of the centre, which is situated out the back of the building – and was once used as stables – Glenn mentioned that, 'this place would be worth investigating'. When I asked why, he said that he, 'gets the impression that heavy footfalls could, or have been heard in there'. Upon chatting to Cindy after our visit, she confirmed to me that she had heard heavy footfalls in this exact location.

She told me, 'They paced back and forth and around the team members while we were in the dark, and we were all perfectly still'. This is something else which we did not know at the time.

Being equipped with our digital diction devices (known as EVP machines), we decided to make a few recordings inside the workshop area. We called out to the atmosphere in the hope that any residing spirits may answer us with their voices, or perhaps make some other noise that we could subsequently record and then analyse. After ten minutes or so, we huddled around the recorder and listened to our recordings. To our total surprise, we all heard a voice that was not that of the investigators present. It simply said, 'Help me.' This particular recording bears striking resemblances to another that I recorded in Durham City back in 2006, whereupon another disembodied voice can be clearly heard speaking the words, 'Can you help me?' Pretty harrowing stuff.

It seems to be the case that there are spirits out there on another level, who are trapped for whatever reason, and are in dire need of help to move on. Why, however, we can only speculate. The evidence for this seems to be most certainly accumulating, and at a steady pace too.

Whatever is going on at the Buffalo Centre in Blyth is truly fascinating, and more work is required there. It seems that there is paranormal activity occurring there on a regular basis, and I for one would love to attempt to get to the bottom of it.

The Burning Man of Barrasford

The Barrasford Arms Hotel, in the village of Barrasford, is said to stand on the site of a much earlier building. This building was also a public house, and over 100 years ago it was razed to the ground after it had caught fire, resulting in the death of one individual – a man. There have been many reports of a 'burning man' who staggers onto the main road that runs past the inn. With his clothes on fire, and his skin burning furiously, this

An artist's impression of the phantom man on fire that has been seen on the road outside of the local pub in Barrasford. (Courtesy of Julie Olley)

Chillingham Castle, Chillingham

apparition is thought to be one of the most horrific spectres one could wish to encounter. After being spotted by witnesses he is said to vanish into thin air; the sound of his screams and shouts still being heard for a short time after, leaving the witnesses shocked and bewildered. One witness, from the village, once reported that he had seen the phantom on fire and noted that the screams that came from the man were 'utterly high pitched and ear shattering'.

Chillingham Castle lies in the wonderful windswept Cheviot Hills of Northumberland, 12–15 miles north-west of Alnwick. It is right on the Border of England and Scotland, and is reputed to be one of the most haunted castles in Europe. It is said to be haunted by Lady Mary Berkeley; she roams the castle looking for her long-lost love, who had ran off with her sister and never returned. Indeed, on dark cold nights, they say you can hear the cries of anguish emanating from within the castle walls.

Chillingham Castle.

The amazing photograph, of the unexplained figure taken by Leonard Butler during one of our many stays in the castle's Grey Apartment. (Courtesy of Leonard Butler)

Chillingham's Topiary Gardens, haunted by the Grey Lady of Chillingham Castle, as seen from the Grey Apartment.

Another spectre seen in the castle is that of 'The Radiant Boy' or 'Blue Boy'. During renovations of the castle, a wall was knocked down and the skeleton of a young boy was found, along with some blue fabric. It is said that the phantom of this ghost is often seen around midnight – glowing blue.

A Grey Lady is said to haunt the Topiary Gardens, which are situated at the side of the castle; and disembodied muttering is often heard coming from the empty library. On many occasions the author has visited the castle and spoken to the owner, Sir Humphrey Wakefield, and he assures me that his ghosts are friendly. Although they are somewhat mischievous, they are most certainly welcome at his home.

I have spent the night at Chillingham Castle on no less than four occasions, and on each of those occasions strange things seemed to occur. Objects were mysteriously moved around in the 'Grey Apartment', the room I had decided to spend the night in. During the course of my stay there, a number of other odd things occurred. A plug that was connected to the wall socket, which was in use at the time, pulled itself out of the wall. We were using a recording device that we had plugged in not ten minutes before. When the recording device went off, and refused to function again, we checked the plug and saw that it had been removed.

A strange photograph was also taken that night by investigator Leonard Butler, showing an anomalous figure, of what could be an apparition, moving across the room. Analysis of the picture has shown it is not a trick of the light, nor is it a lens flare. The picture has not been doctored, and no explanation has ever been found to explain it. We know what it isn't, but we can't say for sure what it is! The strangest thing to occur that night was hearing thunderous bangs coming from inside the apartment, from an open window. We were actually standing out in the courtyard, looking up towards the open window – that we had, incidentally, left closed – when we heard five or six tremendously loud 'thumps'. After returning to the apartment, to find out what these 'raps' were, all was quiet … although the curtains were blowing furiously round in the cold night breeze – it was really odd.

My nights at the infamous Chillingham Castle have proved to be some of the best nights in haunted locations that I have experienced, and if anyone ever tells you the castle is not haunted, they don't know what they are talking about. I know, for sure, that it most certainly is!

Cresswell Tower and Druridge Bay

The village of Cresswell lies on the Northumberland coast south of Druridge Bay – which is also haunted by all accounts – but more of that later. Cresswell itself is a small and sleepy Northumberland village with holiday cottages, a caravan park, a few shops, a few family homes and nothing much else, apart from the haunted tower. The tower, known as Cresswell Tower, is an isolated old building that lies behind a copse of trees on the edge of the Cresswell Caravan Park.

Cresswell Tower was a magnificent home and was once the seat of the Cresswell family. The main house was built alongside a tiny ruin on the north side. The ruin remains, but the house was demolished in the mid-nineteenth century. It is said that another house was built a little west of the tower, named Cresswell Hall. Sadly, this building was demolished in 1937.

Cresswell Tower has a ghost known as the 'Ghost Girl of Cresswell'. She is said to haunt the roof area, although there is no actual roof on the building these days.

Druridge Bay; the ghost here is said to be a Danish prince. Terrible screams are often heard as his gruesome death is audibly replayed here.

The tower, that remains, has now been protected by law to prevent further decay and it is classed as a grade II listed building.

The tower is said to be haunted by a beautiful young girl, who was one of the Cresswell family's daughters. However, during research into this case I discovered there are a number of stories as to how the tower became haunted. She fell in love, it seems, with a prince from Denmark, who made the journey across the North Sea on numerous occasions to rendezvous with the young, smitten girl. On his final trip, to wed the young princess, he moored his boat in the nearby Druridge Bay and made his way ashore. Unfortunately, the princess' brothers were against the love affair, and so they intercepted him on his way to the Cresswell home. A bloody battle ensued, resulting in the brutal death of the Danish prince. The prince's beloved was awaiting his arrival, looking out along the sands from the tower roof. To her horror, she was able to see her lover being butchered right before her eyes. He had come so far, gotten so close, and then was killed on the final leg of his long journey.

It has been suggested that the marriage between the two had already been agreed to, by both families. However, because the Vikings were still seen as deadly enemies by many (although the raids had ceased by this point), the young prince was vilified and paid the ultimate price for his Danish heritage. The wedding was due to have taken place outside of Cresswell Tower, but alas, it was never to be. This is where the tale takes two turns.

One narrative suggests that she refused to eat and subsequently died of starvation in the tower that still remains; the other tale suggests that in her grief she threw herself from its roof. Whatever the truth, the fact remains her ghost has been seen on warm summer evenings longingly looking out from atop the tower. Some say she is still awaiting the return of her lover, and again, some suggest she will haunt the tower until justice is done to the criminals that so savagely took her prince away from her. She is known as Cresswell's 'White Lady'.

As for Druridge Bay, the ghost said to haunt this area of Northumberland is that of the Danish prince – of course. Terrible screams are often heard as his gruesome death is audibly replayed here.

Dilston Castle

Since the Middle Ages, tower houses have appeared all over the world. They are often found in steep hilly areas and other such places with limited access. They were erected in order to defend areas, or 'strategic points', without the use of a sizeable army; in other words, with largely reduced forces. In the same respect, they were also used as private living residences for noblemen and distinguished persons. Dilston Castle, near Corbridge in Northumberland, is one such tower house. Built by Sir William Caxton in the early fifteenth century, on the site of another older tower house, Dilston Castle is now a grade I listed building; it is recorded as a Scheduled Ancient Monument. Dilston Castle, accompanied by its chapel, belongs to the North Pennines Heritage Trust, it is located in the grounds of Dilston College, just off the A695 between Hexham and Corbridge.

The Jacobite rising of 1715, against George I, had failed, and during unrest

Dilston Castle; the ghost of the 3rd Earl of Derwentwater – James Radcliffe – is said to have been seen here on many occasions looking out from one of the upper windows.

thereafter, James Radcliffe – the 3rd Earl of Derwentwater, and the lord of Dilston manor – was beheaded at the Tower of London. The authorities decided to let his headless body be brought back to his native home – whereupon, it is said, his head was sewn back on, before his body was given a decent burial. After his burial, at his family seat at Dilston, his ghost began to be seen in one of Durham Cities old cobbled lanes called South Street. Known in Durham as 'The Thundering Earl', this terrifying spectre has been seen riding on a phantom coach and four, tearing its way along South Street and on many occasions leaving those that saw it quite bewildered, to say the least. Why the Earl of Derwentwater should haunt an old side street in Durham City is anybody's guess. One theory suggests it is because, nearby in New Elvet, stands the County Hotel where at one time – and on that very spot – lived his sister, Lady M. Radcliffe. It is for this reason, and this reason only, that people suggest the ghost of the Earl haunts the streets of Durham. Who knows? They may be correct. No other explanation for his ghost in Durham is forthcoming, or is likely to be, but sightings of his spectre persisted for many years there.

But what about the Earl's castle at Dilston: why doesn't he haunt there? Or the tower of London, where he died, for that matter? Well, he does … if legend is to be believed. James Radcliffe seems to be no different than the likes of Mary Queen of Scots, Anne Boleyn or Henry VIII, in the respect that they too haunt more than one place at a time. His spectre – some people say – can be seen as it looks down from one of the windows at Dilston Castle. Rumours also persist to this day that he and his soldiers can still be heard galloping near the castle as they head off to war.

Dunstanburgh Castle, near Craster

The magnificent ruin of Dunstanburgh Castle is a spectacular place to visit. Set in the ragged surroundings of the Northumberland coastline, this ancient ruin is rumoured to be home to a number of ghosts. Built in around 1313, Dunstanburgh Castle was the idea of Thomas, Earl of Lancaster, who ordered a bastion to be built on this rough and ragged stretch of coastline. Where better to build his edifice than on the cliff tops? It took almost fifteen years to build, and by its completion it was one of the largest and most spectacular castles Northumberland had ever seen.

By then, however, the Earl of Lancaster had been executed for his defeat in the Battle of Boroughbridge, and therefore the castle was taken over by Thomas' cousin, King Edward II.

The castle is renowned for the part it played in the War of the Roses (at which time the castle was held by the Earls of Lancaster), whilst it was being besieged by the Yorkists. The War of the Roses was essentially a series of bitter civil wars between the supporters of the rival houses of Lancaster and York for England's throne, from 1455-1487. They ended with the Lancastrians emerging as victors. A Lancastrian, Henry Tudor (Henry VII) married Elizabeth of York, the daughter of the late Yorkist King Edward IV, in an attempt to reconcile the two factions, and so founded the House of Tudor. The Tudors went on to rule England for the next 116 years or so. Henry's son, Henry VIII succeeded his father after twenty-four years of rule and went on to become one the most famous rulers of all time.

In 1487, after the War of the Roses came to a climax, the castle at Dunstanburgh was left to rot and decay. Being open to the elements on this desolate and barren landscape, it wasn't long before the howling winds and the lashing rains took their toll on what was left of the castle. It now stands empty and derelict, a monument to what was one of the greatest civil wars of the North.

Of course, like most ruined bastions, Dunstanburgh Castle has its fair share of ghosts and legends. Thomas, Earl of Lancaster, is reputed to haunt the ruins of his own castle – he was beheaded following his famous defeat. It is said, by some, that this headless spectre can be seen, with head under his arms (cliché, I know), standing in the area of Lilburn Tower. The wife of Henry VI, Margaret of Anjou, is also reputed to haunt the Lilburn Tower, with her presence being indicated with what has been described as 'a chilling breeze'. I dare say this 'breeze' is felt more often than not since the castle tower is open to the elements and is situated on a cliff top right over the North Sea!

We now enter the realms of folklore and legend and discuss what is probably the most well-known ghost tale that is associated with Dunstanburgh Castle – the ghost of Sir Guy, the Wandering Knight (or the Seeker), and the White Lady of Dunstanburgh. It is said that after seeking adventure for many years he stumbled upon the 'castle on the headland' on a cold and windy night. As he galloped towards it, on his trusty charger, it is said that the great drawbridge was being lowered, and the huge wooden doors to the castle were slowly opening. A voice was then heard to boom out from nowhere and commanded that he should 'enter therein'. As he ventured in, he entered into a magnificent chamber, he was greeted by the sight of a beautiful woman who had been

Yet another beautiful and empty ruin of a castle: the gateway to Dunstanburgh Castle near Craster. This windswept castle is reputedly haunted by a whole plethora of spectres including Thomas, Earl of Lancaster, and Sir Guy, the Seeker.

imprisoned there. She had long black hair and a flowing white dress; she was the most beautiful woman he had ever laid eyes upon. Suddenly, an apparitional and cloudy arm materialised from nowhere and in the hand was a sword, and a horn. Guy was told that he should choose one of these objects but he should choose wisely, as one of them would secure the release of the beautiful woman.

Had he chosen the sword, he would have been given the opportunity to fight for, and free the woman that was being held captive there. This, in effect, would be proving his worth as a valiant warrior. However, he chose the horn and blew it (in the literal and metaphorical sense).

Choosing the horn indicated that he lacked valour and the blowing of the horn would be seen as summoning assistance. As soon as the horn was blown, Sir Guy found himself outside of the castle lying down in the mud, cold and wet. Many attempts were made by Guy to get back inside the castle but to no avail.

It is said that on cold and stormy nights, the beautiful lady in white haunts Dunstanburgh Castle awaiting the arrival of a new knight or an adventurer whose choice will be the sword. However, it is said that Sir Guy also haunts the castle too – again, on stormy nights. He is said to be a tormented and restless spirit that is forever seeking the beautiful lady in white.

The Lilburn Tower at Dunstanburgh. It is said, by some, that Thomas, Earl of Lancaster's headless spectre can be seen with head under his arms standing in the area of Lilburn Tower, as clichéd as it sounds.

I remember a few years ago visiting Dunstanburgh Castle on a day out. I had wanted to visit the castle for a long time to photograph the ruins and its views, from high on the cliff tops. We had parked the car at Embleton, which is a small village a mile or so from the castle, and made our way along the sands. It was a foggy day, as it had been all morning – you could not see 10 yards ahead of yourself. I thought my photographic opportunities were well and truly scuppered, due to the dense mist, but decided to enjoy the day regardless. Being one of my first visits to the ruin in a long time, I did not know how long it would take to reach the castle, as we meandered along the sand dunes and by the golf course. It seemed to take forever to get there and I even wondered if we were heading in the right direction.

Suddenly, after what seemed like a life-time of walking, we found ourselves at the foot of a steep hill. Perched high on the top of it was Lilburn Tower, just visible through the mist. As we progressed towards the main gateway to the castle, avoiding the giant cow-pats as we went, something strange seemed to occur. It was patently obvious that the closer we got to the castle, the more the fog seemed to lift! By the time we arrived, and had made our way in, the fog had completely lifted and magnificent views could be enjoyed from all angles, in all directions. I happily snapped away with my camera, taking an abundance of dramatic and very scenic photographs. After spending about an hour or so in the castle, using up the last frame on my roll of thirty-six, we decided to head back to the car for some sandwiches and a drink. As soon as we left the castle entrance, and made our way back along the rugged path toward

Lilburn Tower, the fog enveloped the castle once more, shrouding it in a thick dense mist which stayed for the rest of the day. It was really odd. I am not saying this was paranormal, of course, but it seemed mighty coincidental that the fog had lifted just at the right time, and then shrouded the ruins again just as we left, giving me enough time to see and photograph the castle.

Edlingham Castle

Edlingham Castle, near Edlingham village, was never meant to be a 'castle', so to speak. It developed that way following many different owners additions; refining it, knocking parts down and rebuilding it, until it was eventually given 'castle' status. When it was officially declared a castle is unclear but as the years passed and and the building became more of a garrison, its reputation as a castle was confirmed.

In 1296, Sir William de Felton fortified the house. Back in those troubled times, raids and Border-land sieges between the Scots and English were commonplace. So this fortification was borne of necessity, considering the castle's geographical location. This one-time, two-storey home, which was originally built by John de Edlingham in the twelfth century, was abandoned in the mid-1600s with the lower sections of the 'castle' being used to house farmland animals. By now the building was crumbling, and it rapidly fell into a state of disrepair. As another 300 years elapsed, the castle suffered massively from further decay and disuse. Years of driving rains and moor-land gale-force winds tend to take their toll, and Edlingham paid the price for the neglect it received.

Sadly, it was never rebuilt to its former glory, but almost 800 years on work was undertaken to make these ancient ruins safe for those people who wanted to visit the derelict shell. In 1978, English Heritage carried out the much-needed work to preserve these magnificent ruins and succeeded in stopping the remainder of the castle from collapsing. Not only did they save the ruin, but also. in all the likelihood, they saved lives too.

The castle ruin is said to be haunted, of course, with strange and eerie noises being heard coming from the ruins late at night. Of course these 'noises' may well have natural explanations, but some folk would beg to differ – namely those that have actually heard them! Strange, eerie spheres of luminescent light have been seen flickering around the ruined shell too. Not your normal everyday 'light orbs', I might add, but real 'visible with the naked eye' glowing balls of energy (for want of a better word). No one knows what they are, but some say they are the residual energies that are left over from long-dead souls – maybe soldiers from the Border Wars? Flickering shadows are seen in the ruins quite often too – during the day and the night – and quite often visitors are said to feel their clothes being tugged by invisible hands as though something – or someone – wants their attention.

But what is the cause of these alleged paranormal phenomena? Are there any tales that could account for the ghostly goings-on? Any tragedies that may have occurred there that could have left their mark on the area? Apart from the obvious Border Wars and sieges – which would have resulted in lots of bloodshed and gruesome deaths – there is a tale that concerns a local woman, known as 'the Edlingham witch'.

The Edlingham witch was known as Margaret Stothard – according to author Rob Kirkup – and resided in the Edlingham

The main entrance at Edlingham Castle.
(Courtesy of Suzanne Hitchinson)

The majestic ruin of Edlingham Castle in the far reaches of Northumberland. The haunting centres around the tale of the Edlingham Witch, otherwise known as Margaret Stothard. Strange things have also occurred here over the years, including mysterious ghostly footfalls being heard, and dark shadows that flit around the ruin at dusk. (Courtesy of Suzanne Hitchinson)

area around 300 years ago. She was a nice woman, by all accounts, and used her powers and potions to help people. By today's standards she would be considered as a herbalist of some sort. Some say she was also a gifted medium, which of course led to her being labelled the witch in the first place. Magic potions, seeing into the future, and reading people's minds was not really classed as 'normal' (it still isn't today), so despite the fact she was considered a good woman, she was also considered to be in league with the Devil. To cut a long story short, she was arrested and tried for witchcraft in 1682, with the sad thing being that those she helped and healed were the very people who testified against her! The trial verdict was 'unproven', and thankfully, unlike many other witches at that time – or at least, so-called witches – she walked free. An interesting tale to say the least but it sheds no light on the haunting of the castle …

To find out whether the castle was haunted or not, I needed to speak to people who had first-hand experience of 'odd happenings' at the ruins. Sure, the castle has its reputation – as most castles do – but does it really house denizens of the other world, and if so, just who are they? Well, as it happens, I managed to track down a few people who experienced ghostly phenomena during their visits there. One person claims to have experienced something 'scary' on just about every visit he has made there. His name is John Triplow and is a Northumberland based paranormal investigator who has investigated many sites in the region; he is a thorough researcher. What he told us is rather disturbing, to say the least:

> For whatever reason I've always preferred investigating the lesser-known locale. Of course, Chillingham Castle and the likes are all great places to visit, but, sadly, they always seem to fall short when it boils down to truly *bona-fide* paranormal activity. That is not to say they're not haunted, by any means – but I can only speak as I have found.

One place that isn't as well known, yet which has left me completely dumbfounded on several occasions in the past, is the old ruin of Edlingham Castle. On two separate occasions I have witnessed stone-throwing (actually performed on request during one visit), without any apparent signs of human intervention or trickery. On another occasion I clearly heard a sound that resembled the stamping of feet on stone – although everyone present was accounted for at the time. In truth, the list goes on – it really is a mysterious little place.

However, the strangest occurrence that happened in regard to Edlingham was when a fellow researcher, and good friend of mine, Gail Ward, emailed over a series of pictures while I was reviewing the evidence after one such investigation at the castle.

Amongst those photographs was an image of what appeared to be a small boy standing next to an old fireplace, wearing something that looked similar to an old-fashioned, tricorn hat. However, what intrigued us more than anything was what happened when we returned to Edlingham to take a series of photographs of the fireplace, in an attempt to explain the mysterious anomaly. We ended up even more baffled than we had been originally.

When we inspected the fireplace, it was clear that there was a stone present that was almost identical to the shape and diameter of the said 'tricorn hat'. Mystery solved, then – or so we thought, anyway.

Yet, after comparing the two images, it became increasingly obvious that what we believed had caused the simulacrum in the first place actually gave the picture some stunning credibility rather than explaining it away completely. The stone clearly points in the opposite direction from the 'tricorn'. This led us to conclude that whatever was standing to the right of the fireplace that night was more likely to have been obscuring the wall and not the wall generating a simulative image. So does that mean it's a ghost? Well, it could well be, but we just don't know.

Suzanne Hitchinson is a very good friend of mine, who I have known for many years now, and she too experienced 'odd stuff' at Edlingham. I asked her to tell me all about it and she went on to say:

I have visited the castle on a number of occasions and have sensed many different spirits there. The one who seems to come forward the most is a female spirit around about the age of twenty. I have communicated with her a few times and she went on to tell me how she was a medicine woman from a nearby village; she was a frequent visitor to the castle, and was called for to cure the ailments of the people there with her natural ways.

The place has a very eerie feel to it and you often feel as if you are being watched by someone or something. I have caught glimpses of shadows that seem to play hide and seek, and have heard, on occasions, mumblings as if a conversation was taking place somewhere within the ruins; no one else was there, of course. The place is steeped in psychic energy and is definitely worth a visit if you are ever up on Alnwick moors.

Elsdon Gibbet, Elsdon

William Winter murdered a woman named Margaret Crozier in August 1791 in Elsdon, which is only a few miles from Otterburn in Northumberland. For this crime he was tried and hanged in Newcastle; his lifeless body was then taken to the scene of his crime, where it was hung up in a gibbet to act as a deterrent to other would-be criminals. It is said that he haunts this lonely, barren and cold moor, staring regretfully from the roadside near his gibbet post. A gibbet post still stands there up on the moors at Elsdon, and is known as 'Winter's Gibbet' or 'The Elsdon Gibbet'. It has a wooden head that hangs from it. It is an eerie, chilling sight that would unnerve the most sceptical of people should they stumble across it on a foggy or misty evening. Legend has it that if one suffers from toothache, you can take a splinter from the gibbet post and rub it on the infected area, whereupon the toothache will shortly disappear.

There is also another ghost that is said to haunt the barren wasteland of the moors, in this neck of the north-east of England, and it is a spectre known as 'The Brown Man'. The story goes that two Newcastle men were out and about on the Elsdon Moors, partaking in a spot of hunting. After a while they decided to rest, so they sat down near a little river (or burn), that flowed through a quiet and verdant parcel of land. They took a drink from the burn and wiped their mouths down. As they got up to continue their hunting, they both noticed something strange. They described it as a 'little brown human-being, half the size of a normal man'. He had red frizzy hair and the expression on his face gave the two men the impression that he was very annoyed; he was gazing at them with malevolent eyes.

It is said that the little brown man spoke to the men and asked them if they knew who he was, to which they replied 'The Lord of the Manor', and then offered the little brown man all the game they had killed, thinking it was that which he wanted. The brown man refused the game and explained that he lived in the woods and ate nothing but berries, nuts and mushrooms. He then asked the two men if they fancied some of his hospitality at his abode in the woods. The two men looked at each other to discuss what on earth they should do, and when they looked back he had completely vanished

An odd postscript tells us that within one year of talking to the little brown man, the elder of the two men had died of a severe and on-going virus. Some say that the death had supernatural causes, and that the little brown man was responsible for his death. Because of this, the spectre of this small, brown dwarf-like creature has been feared ever since. They say if you ever visit the Elsdon Moors and come across this evil little sprite, do not engage in conversation with him as death will surely follow.

One night, back in March 2010, Mark Winter (who claims to be a descendant of the infamous William) and I paid a visit to the gibbet post to see if we could 'experience' anything remotely odd, or indeed supernatural. It had always been a bit of an ambition of mine to hold a vigil, through the night, under Winter's Gibbet, with video cameras and dictation machines at the ready. It was a bitterly cold evening, and there was not a cloud in sight, making the dark night sky a total wonder to behold. In fact, I have never seen so many stars in my life – it was truly breathtaking. The night was unusually silent and still, considering we were on the top of what is normally a windswept moor – we had perfect condi-

Standing alone on the windswept moors of Northumberland stands Winter's Gibbet post. William Winter was hung in a gibbet cage after his part in the gruesome murder of Margaret Crozier in August 1791.

tions. The only thing that broke the silence was the sound of our feet as we made our way to the gibbet post.

Of course, we all know that the post that stands there today is not the original from which Winter was gibbeted – it is a replica. The real gibbet post stood a yard or so to the right. Its original base stone (complete with the hole in which the post nestled) is visible to this day.

All in all, Mark and I spent a good few hours in and around the gibbet post, and on the road from where William's ghost is said to be seen. The cold eventually got the better of us, and we were forced back into

the warmth of the car. Upon checking the tapes and recordings we'd made, we found nothing – still, we weren't too disappointed, as we'd expected nothing less. Although we were unsuccessful in obtaining any results from our EVP machines and video cameras, John Triplow has had a more fruitful experience. John, as you have read, told me all about his exploits at Edlingham Castle and is well-versed in ghost hunting in Northumberland.

I asked him about the gibbet at Elsdon and what follows is John's thoughts of the area in general:

The story of Winter's Gibbet is one that has both intrigued and fascinated me for many years. When I was about ten years old I remember taking a clipping from a local newspaper article that was coupled as an advertisement for a book written by Clive Kristen called *Ghostly Trails of Northumberland*. One story that was highlighted in the article made reference to a grisly, 200-year-old murder that had taken place near the quaint village of Elsdon in Northumberland, and the subsequent execution of a local gang member named William Winter.

But what really fascinated me about this tale was the fact that Winter's ghost is still believed to haunt the woodland, which is close to where his lifeless corpse was displayed on a gibbet, as a macabre reminder to anyone who wished to replicate such a horrific crime. It is said that, on certain nights, the disembodied screams of the murderer's tormented soul can still be heard deep within the forest.

Years later, once I had associated myself with paranormal research, Winter's Gibbet was indeed high on the list of places I wanted to investigate. So, on 30 May 2009, along with several members of Supernatural Investigations of Ghosts in Northumbria, I decided to spend the night in Harwood Forest to see if there was any truth in the claims that were being made.

As the night wore on, nothing particularly strange had happened. We had walked about a mile down the road from the campsite but decided to head back as we felt there was nothing to be gained from walking any further. Once we were back in the relative comfort of the site, I decided to review some of the recordings that we had made throughout the course of that night. Settling myself down on a log next to the warmth of the fire, I began to listen to the recordings. After about a minute or so I was shocked to hear a harsh, male voice burst from the speakers of the Olympus digital recorder. Judging by the look on my colleague's face, he too had heard exactly what I had. Initially, it was difficult to decipher what was being said, so I knew we would have to wait until the following day to review the evidence efficiently.

When I arrived back home, I rushed over to the PC and uploaded the recorded files. I honed in on the section that contained the voice and proceeded to increase the volume and reduced some of the annoying hiss from the file. To my utter amazement I could hear what sounded like a male voice speaking to two females. For all the world, it sounded to me like the male voice was asking, 'Do you think they'll take the three of us?' The first female responds with, 'I don't know.' Then, again, a second, softer female voice responds with, 'I don't know'. What I find so intriguing about this is that it fits the bill perfectly when you consider William Winter had two female accomplices. Of course, we can't be certain that we have recorded the disembodied voices of Winter and the Clark sisters, but I think it makes sense that it would be them. Who knows, it may well be!

Make of that what you will …

Featherstone Castle, Near Haltwhistle

Close to the small town of Haltwhistle, in Northumberland, stands the magnificent Featherstone Castle. The castle dates from the early 1400s; Featherstonehaugh, the family, for whom the castle is named, still resided there up until the eighteenth century. The ghosts of Featherstone Castle are very well-known amongst the region's paranormal experts and date back to the late 1600s. The ghosts which are said to reside there are that of a bridal party who went out one night and never returned. After the arranged marriage of Abigail Featherstonehaugh, by her father, the Baron Featherstonehaugh, the wedding party set out on a traditional deer hunt, to celebrate the occassion. The Baron, who had duties to attend to at the castle, stayed behind and waited in anticipation for their return. During his time at the castle, he prepared the huge feast for all the wedding party and their guests.

It was approaching midnight, by which time the Baron was becoming worried as the party had yet to return. While sitting

Featherstone Castle, near Haltwhistle, in 1981. Dating from the early 1400s, this castle was the scene of an amazing ghostly bridal procession. (Courtesy of Newcastle Libraries and Information Service)

An alternate view of Featherstone Castle. (Courtesy of Newcastle Libraries and Information Service)

at the table, racked with worry, he was overjoyed to hear the horses clip-clopping their way over the wooden drawbridge and returning home, or so he thought. He ran to the castle entrance to greet the wedding party, but was stopped in his tracks, aghast, at the sight of his transparent blood-stained daughter and her wedding party, who were making their way into the castle. They marched straight through the furniture, and then on, through the castle wall.

Abigail had not wanted to marry the suitor that her father had lined up for her; she was married against her will. This was a common occurrence in those days, with a great deal of arranged marriages ending in tragedy. It is thought that the man that she really loved, a member of a local family named Ridley, had lain in wait with a huge gang of murderous colleagues, and had purposely attacked the wedding party. No mercy was shown by Ridley and his rabble – not even for his betrothed lover – and everyone was slain on that savage and brutal night. It is said that on the anniversary of the tragedy – some say 17 January – the phantom bridal party may briefly be seen marching into the castle – silent and blood splattered. An annual reminder of the tragic wedding day.

However, one thing puzzles me about Baron Featherstonehaugh's sighting. How did he hear them approach – as they crossed the drawbridge – when they were silent once he'd seen them? It is as though the two halves of the bridal party's return are opposite to each other – heard and not seen (on the drawbridge), then seen and not heard (entering the castle). Answers on a postcard …

Two other spectres are said to reside at the castle also. One of the ghosts is an unknown woman who has been seen, on occasions, as she meanders along the long corridors of the castle. She is said to wear a long green dress, but when approached she vanishes into thin air. The other sad spectre is thought to be the victim of a starvation, who perished in the castle. His moans and groans, which reverberated around the halls, are still believed to emanate throughout the castle. They are sure to send chills down the spines of those who hear them.

Flodden Field Phantoms

The Battle of Branxton Moor, otherwise known as the Battle of Flodden Field, was probably the last medieval battle to take place in this country. It took place on 9 September 1513, and it was a great victory for the English. Late on that fateful September afternoon, over 10,000 men died (mainly Scots) – it took just two hours. The Scots, under King James IV, had invaded England in an effort to divert the English army that was – at that time – fighting in France against King Louis XII during the War of the League of Cambrai (1508–1516). The Scots were met by the army of the Earl of Surrey, Thomas Howard. In terms of actual numbers, it is purported that the Battle of Flodden Field was the biggest battle to have been fought between these two warring countries.

King James of Scotland was reported to have died that day after fighting bravely; his body was later said to have been inspected, or identified, by Sir William Scott, and Lord Dacre – an unenviable task. The butchered body of the King was said to have been so horribly damaged and disfigured that it was barely recognisable at all. One of his hands had been severed and and his throat had been cut. He was nevertheless identified as the King, and his body was wrapped in his country's flag. It was subsequently

The commemorative Flodden monument, which stands at Flodden Field
in memory of all those that perished during the battle. This picture is from
around 1911. (Courtesy of Newcastle Libraries and Information Service)

embalmed, and was then taken to London to be buried in a pauper's grave.

A lot of people quite often mistake the area of Flodden as the actual battle site, but the battle actually took place closer to the village of Branxton. Lying south of Branxton was an area known as 'Flodden Edge', and it was here that the Scots had stationed themselves prior to the battle. Using the murder of one Robert Kerr, who had been killed by John Heron in 1508, as an excuse to wage a war against the English, King James invaded Northumbria with an army of just under 30,000 men. It was one of the biggest mistakes ever made in Scottish warfare, with the loss of thousands of men – including many of their church leaders, just about all of their nobility and, of course, their King.

Are there ghosts at Flodden Field? Well, some folk suggest there most certainly are. Rob Kirkup's book, *Ghostly Northumberland*, says that there have been many reports of the chilling sounds of the battle, as though it is being re-enacted. The clash of swords, the screams of the fighting men, and the moans and groans of dying soldiers are all said to be heard – most often, in the 'dead of night'. He goes on to say that the nearby road, the A697, is also a location for a ghost sighting. The phantoms of soldiers have allegedly been seen walking silently across the lane.

Clive Kristen, however, tells us in his book *Ghostly Trails of Northumbria* that there is only one single phenomenon that has been reported there: bits of old clothes, and fragments of cloth, have been seen to flap around in the breezes. As they are approached they seem to fade somewhat, before disappearing altogether. One presumes he is talking about the remnants of the soldier's battle-attire that have been ripped from their bodies during the battle, and have lain, on the field, alongside their rotten corpses. This is a most strange, yet interesting, phenomenon.

Gilsland's Ghost Boy, Gilsland

Many years ago I investigated an old public house in the village of Gilsland, and had quite an unnerving night, experiencing all kinds of paranormal phenomena. Light bulbs blew, knocks and taps were heard, footfalls thumped their way across empty rooms, and the apparition of a man, in a rail uniform, was allegedly seen by some observers on our investigation. But it is not the haunted pub I wish to discuss, however, but rather the ghost of a young lad, known as 'the sobbing child'.

Gilsland has a ruined castle and a Roman wall, and according to writer and ghost-hunter Jack Hallum it also boasts a ghost that haunts both. Described as a 'harrowing spectre', the phantom of a young child – no older than six years old – is said to inhabit the area around the aforementioned locales. If you ever visit the area, on a day out, be grateful if you only feel the touch of his icy cold hand on yours. It is said that if you see the wretched, scruffy youngster, bad luck will befall you. If you hear the pathetic voice of a child saying, 'Cold for ever more', and sobbing at the same time, through chattering teeth, beware – he is close by.

The cold lad, or 'cauld lad', of Gilsland is said to be the shade of an orphaned boy who, many years ago, was the victim of his greedy uncle. The child was to inherit a massive fortune at the age of twenty-one, but when his parents died he was entrusted into the care of his relative. He was mistreated from the off, being housed in the dungeons and never fed adequately. If the boy was to somehow meet his untimely end … accidentally, the money would go to

An artist's impression of the cold and sobbing ghost boy that has been seen in the area of Gilsland. (Courtesy of Julie Olley)

The Eagle Pub, Blyth

The Eagle Public House, in Newsham in Blyth, is not the sort of tavern where one would expect to see ghosts. This pub is a fairly modern edifice. It was built no more than forty years ago – around the 1970s, I am told – and it reminds me of these new-style fashionable pubs and drinking houses that are cropping up all over the place. Like other pubs, similar to this, it looks very large from the outside and looks even larger from within. Decked out with TV screens, pool tables, dart boards and a huge amount of seating areas, the pub is an ideal locale for spending Saturday afternoons with a good pint, watching sport or simply relaxing.

The main bar area is all wooded, and does have a 'certain feel to it', even during the day. The function rooms have wonderful low ceilings, with huge heavy-looking wooden beams criss-crossing their expanse. If the pub is trying to create an 'olde-world' feel, then it is doing something right. Upstairs there is another function room and the owner's living area.

Originally built for the Scottish & Newcastle Breweries, the Eagle has seen a good number of tenants and occupants over the four decades it has been open.

While the Eagle Public House is not the sort of place where one would expect to see ghosts, you can never say never. Anywhere can be haunted, as this story will show. The owner and current land-lady, Stephanie Bariana, seems to think that her pub may be 'ghosted' after a number of strange goings-on have reputedly been experienced by herself, her punters, and her members of staff.

As it happens, my colleague Mark Winter has a sister that works at this pub and she has experienced some of the strange phenomena for herself. Claire Rutherford (neé Winter),

his new carer. To make sure the lad would never get his rightful inheritance, his uncle took him out – barely dressed – onto the nearby common, in sub-zero conditions and in a thick blizzard, leaving him there to find his own way back to the castle. The uncle ran away from the boy, so that he couldn't catch up; he made sure he himself was well-wrapped up in long coats and furs to keep warm.

Of course, the boy had no chance of finding his way back to the castle, and he therefore died of cold and starvation out on the desolate moors. He was found dead, huddled up in a ball, near some rocks on the moors. It was clear, to those that found him, that he had crawled there in search of shelter from the ice-cold winds and snow.

tells me that, on one occasion, while alone in the kitchen, she heard the distinct sound of a voice whisper in her ear. The voice simply said her name, 'Claire'. A person hearing their name whispered is not uncommon in haunted locations, and I know of many other cases where this has occurred. It is usually – and rather luckily – when the person in question is in the premises on their own and can categorically state that the voice they heard was inexplicable.

The apparition of a man has been seen inside the pub on occasions, by a number of different people. The owner, Stephanie, her stepfather, John, and some of the pub clientele have reported him too. He was said to have been seen wearing black trousers and a long dark coat. He slowly ambles down the main stairwell in the pub before drifting into the main function room. Upon inspection of the function room, however, no one is ever found and all the entrances and exits are always locked tight. This ghost has been seen on two separate occasions

in the last few years; one occasion saw the specre being witnessed by two people at same time. I, for one, would love to know who he is. Other strange paranormal-like occurrences are reported at the pub too, which include the classic 'haunted location' symptoms. These are mainly doors that open and close on their own, and objects moving around on their own (glasses, etc). In April 2010 a customer, known as Larry, was sitting enjoying his pint, when, suddenly, the glass he was drinking from exploded on the table right before his eyes. As he'd only taken a sip, the majority ended up on Larry's lap.

The sound of a man coughing is regularly heard in the 'area' where Larry sits – only when there is no one sitting there, of course. Talking and eerie whispering has been heard by the staff late at night, when the building is closed up and no one is around; unexplained thumps and knocks have been heard by several people on different occasions also. Very interesting for

The Eagle pub in Blyth. The pub is not actually that old, but ghosts seem hell bent on inhabiting the place nonetheless.

a place that you wouldn't expect 'to be haunted'.

I visited the pub with Mark Winter one night, in May 2010, and was given the full low-down of what had been going on there. We took a comprehensive tour of the premises and I was astounded by its underground tunnel system and its many hidden passages and walled-up rooms, which most people are unaware of. This pub reminds me of an 'old manor house' style of building, where priests would hide in their walls when the King's men came knocking. Why a building that was built in the 1970s should have these amazing nooks and crannies is anybody's guess, but it does – and the building is much better for it.

By the time you read this book the investigations will have been carried out and full reports of my findings will hopefully be in preparation for full public release.

The Hexham Heads, Hexham

This story dates back to 1972, when two young brothers named Robson, from Hexham in Northumberland, experienced a very startling and harrowing experience after digging in their garden. During their excavations, they came across two stone objects, both round in shape; they were about the size of a grapefruit, or a large apple. When they examined the find more closely, they realised they had unearthed what appeared to be a pair of carved heads. Where they came from, or from when, no one knows – this feature of the case is yet to be resolved.

A few nights after their find, their neighbour, Ellen Dodd, was in her home watching televison in her bedroom with her family when a creature entered the bedroom. The creature was a 'half-man,

half-beast', and, despite the terrified screams of Ellen and her family, it paid them no heed. Instead, it turned calmly before making its way downstairs. When they eventually plucked up the courage to venture downstairs and have a look around, they found their front door wide open. It seems the creature had exited the house.

Dr Anne Ross, an academic, took possession of these mysterious heads and kept them in her home. A few nights later, at about 2 a.m., she woke from her slumber feeling 'cold and frightened, for no apparent reason'. Then she saw something at her door that she described as 'truly disturbing':

> It was about six feet high, slightly stooping, and it was black, against the white door, and it was half animal and half man. The upper part, I would have said, was a wolf, and the lower part was human... It was covered with a kind of black, very dark fur. It went out and I just saw it clearly. Then it disappeared, and something made me run after it – a thing I wouldn't normally have done, but I felt compelled to run after it. I got out of bed and I ran, and I could hear it going down the stairs. Then it disappeared towards the back of the house.

This was put down to a bad dream, but some some time later she arrived home with her husband, archaeologist Richard Feacham, to find their teenage daughter, Berenice, in great distress. Berenice told her parents that when she entered the house, through the front door, she saw a huge, black shape dashing down the stairwell.

Half way down, the beast effortlessly vaulted over the banister rail and landed in the hallway, on its padded feet. Perhaps wisely, Ross passed on the custodianship of the heads to others and they eventually found their way to the British Museum. Here also, however, they were said to be responsible for some rather disturbing events of a paranormal nature and they were taken off show. The mystery of the Hexham Heads was never solved, although there have long been rumours that the beast-like apparition that seemed to accompany them was connected to an enigmatic creature known as the Allendale Wolf.

Milecastle 42; Hadrian's Wall – the Ghost of Lucius

The stretch of Hadrian's Wall, between Housesteads Roman Fort and Greenhead, is one of my favourite places in Northumberland.

The sections of wall that run through this beautiful part of Northumberland are some of the best preserved along the entire length of this magnificent Roman structure. On many occasions I have had the pleasure of hiking along them, and one never tires of visiting this historic site. One of the most breathtaking sections – and probably the most photographed – is a few miles west of Housesteads Fort and is known as Sycamore Gap. Sycamore Gap was made famous in the 1991 classic film, *Robin Hood: Prince of Thieves* starring Kevin Costner and Morgan Freeman.

In all my years of ghost hunting and research, I had never heard of any ghost tales that were associated with Hadrian's Wall. I always presumed there were ghosts attached to it, but never knew exactly what – or, more to the point, where – they were. Then I read the account of Milecastle 42, at Cawfields. Recorded in Clive Kristen's admirable book, *Ghost Trails of Northumbria,* the story goes that a Roman soldier who was garrisoned at Milecastle 42 fell in love with a local woman. The two lovers, Lucius (the soldier) and Eanfritha (the woman) were said to have met up during Lucius' patrolling of Milecastle 42. The local woman was

Hadrian's Wall; an exceptionally beautiful part of Northumberland and not without a ghost or two.

Sycamore Gap on Hadrian's Wall between Housesteads Roman Fort and Cawfields.

Sloping down towards Cawfields where Milecastle 42 stands. (Photograph courtesy of Gail Ward)

of a duplicitous nature, it seems; she did not feel the same way as Lucius and was simply keeping him distracted while her brother climbed over the wall and stole Roman goods.

Her brother, called Ethelric, eventually became cocksure and arrogant to the point where he was boasting about his successful endeavours as a professional thief. Ultimately, he was caught because of it. Realising there was no way out for him – after trying unsuccessfully to deny it – he decided to selfishly implicate poor Lucius. Although Lucius had nothing to do with the thefts, his lack of attention as a guardsman was obviously brought to the attention of his superiors. Lucius now faced two options – dismissal or death. Being faced with the disgrace of his dismissal, combined with the fact that his so-called lover had deceived him, he decided the only way out was to fall upon his own sword. Unfortunately, however, he bodged that up too, missing all his vital organs with the sword. So he was left incapacitated, in agony, unable to do just about anything.

Eanfritha heard about what had happened. Feeling inescapable remorse, she immediately rushed to his side. After reconciling, Lucius decided that he did not want to die after all, and so fought hard for his life. It seemed that for a while Lucius was going to make a full recovery, but fate then played a cruel hand: after contracting a fever, due to an infection in his gaping wound, Lucius passed away. Eanfritha was devastated, of course.

It is the forlorn ghost of Lucius that is said to walk the wall at Milecastle 42, even though 2,000 years have elapsed. Some

An artist's impression of Lucius, the Roman soldier ghost that has been seen at Milecastle 42. (Courtesy of Julie Olley)

Mitford Castle, Near Morpeth

The village of Mitford lies on the River Wansbeck a mile or two west of Morpeth. Its castle, Mitford Castle, was built around 1138 by one William Bertram. Sadly, not much remains of the fortress today, but what does remain is classed as a Scheduled Ancient Monument and is a grade I listed building. Interestingly, the castle was said to have been built with the only five-sided keep in the whole of England.

In 2005, English Heritage donated £16,000 (in the form of two separate grants) into a fund that was set up to help preserve and maintain what is left of the castle. The castle, in its dreadful state, after nearly 1,000 years of most turbulent history, was on the verge of collapse. Painstaking work began by removing large tree stumps and other fauna that were undermining the remaining walls and making them very unstable. Once the trees and large roots were eventually removed, the castle stones were replaced where they had been previously. You would never have known they had even been moved. It would have been a dreadful shame to lose the remains of this wonderful old ruin after all it has been through over the years. Sieges, battles, fires: you name it, Mitford has seen it. It would also have been a darn shame to lose the one and only ghost – as terrifying as it is – that is said to inhabit these ancient walls. Ghosts quite often disappear with buildings once they are demolished, although there are cases where they are said to stay on and haunt the new premises. Had Mitford not been restored to the extent it has been, we may have lost its ghost forever. I, for one, am glad the castle remains.

These desolate and eerie ruins sit, in stark contrast to their surroundings, atop a large hillock with bushes and trees growing up

say he is foolishly waiting for his lover Eanfritha, while others suggest he walks the wall in punishment for neglecting his guard duties – no one knows for sure. Clive Kristen tells us that the ghost of Lucius, presents an eerie and strange vision', as he, 'walks on the original wall level and so appears to be floating on a cushion of air'. He ties up the story by saying, 'He is also one of the rare breed of ghosts whose appearances take place most frequently during daylight hours'.

The ruin of Mitford Castle near Morpeth. Haunted by an extremely harrowing spectre and strange lights that seem to flit about in the dead of night.

A ruined doorway inside the shell of Mitford Castle; a possible location for the scene that was observed here in 1934.

An artist's impression of the frightening spectre, seen here with the head in his hands, and with his weapon drawn. (Courtesy of Julie Olley)

couple of young lads were playing inside the ruins. Suddenly – it is said – the boys stopped dead in their tracks as a loud and harrowing scream reverberated around the ruined castle. A soldier (some suggest a warrior, but let's not split hairs), then stepped out from nowhere and confronted the two youngsters. In one hand he carried a huge weapon; in the other hand, a severed head! If you think that was bad enough, wait until you hear what happened next. Suddenly, the harrowing, unearthly scream, came once more, but it was not the phantom soldier that wailed – it was the severed head! If the youngsters were not going to run before, they sure did now … leaving a cloud of dust, as you may well imagine; I mean, who wouldn't?

I asked a number of locals if there had been any new sightings of ghosts or 'harrowing screams' coming from the castle at night. Screams are often heard here, in the dead of night, but I was told, 'the only screams we get round here are from the foxes.' One Morpeth man told me, however, that while out walking his dogs, late on a winter's night, he noticed some rather odd lights flitting about the ruins. When I asked him what kind of lights they were, he said, 'I dunno … just lights. They didn't half spook the dogs though'.

What the lights were that were flitting around the ruins is anybody's guess. Teenagers messing around? A firefly? Fairyfolk? Or perhaps the mysterious lights were of long-dead soldiers, who once fought over this one-time magnificent fortress? One thing is for sure: if anyone sees more mysterious lights floating about the ruins, I would love to hear about it.

all around them. On the approach to the castle itself, one gets that awful feeling that you are being watched – maybe there is a malevolent spirit keeping guard over the ruins. The ghost of Mitford Castle is still said to lurk in the crumbling ruins, perhaps waiting for unsuspecting visitors to run into him. I ventured around these ruins back in May 2010 on a blisteringly hot day hoping that the ghost would appear for me; alas, it did not. I was taken aback by the sheer size of the castle site and the thickness of the outer walls; they really don't make buildings the way they used to!

The last sighting of Mitford's ghost was said to have occurred in 1934, when a

Haughton Castle and the ghost of Archie Armstrong, near Barrasford

Haughton Castle is a privately-owned castle, located near Barrasford. It dates back to the fourteenth century, when it was known to be a fortified bastion. It was owned by the Widringtons and our ghost tale revolves around the then lord of Haughton, Sir Thomas De Widdrington.

Imagine, if you will, being locked-up in a small dungeon and being given nothing to eat. Imagine if, out of thirst and hunger, you were forced to eat your own flesh and drink your own blood in an effort to survive. Well, this was allegedly the fate of Archie Armstrong, after Sir Thomas De Widdrington had him arrested and thrown in the castle's deepest and darkest cell. It is thought that Archie Armstrong was in league with one Lord Darce, of the Liddlesdale clans, and by all accounts they were up to no good. The landowners had petitioned to have something done about the scoundrels, who were upsetting their lands, and the full document was given to Sir Thomas De Widdrington so he could deliver it to Cardinal Wolsey in York.

Before Sir Thomas left for York, Archie Armstrong was apprehended and jailed. After three days, Sir Thomas arrived in York and realised that he held the only key to the dungeon where Archie was being held. It dawned on him that since his arrest, the prisoner had been given no food or water. Before handing over the petition to the cardinal, he mounted his horse and galloped off, at speed, to return to Haughton Castle. He hoped to get back before the prisoner died of malnutrition. Of course, it took another three days to reach the castle, in which time one of Sir Thomas' horses had collapsed and died of exhaustion. A

Haughton Castle in 1940. Haunted by the ghost of Archie Armstrong. (Courtesy of the Newcastle Libraries and Information Service)

second horse brought him the rest of the way. Sir Thomas had had no rest either, and he too was close to collapse.

On arriving at Haughton Castle he made his way to the dungeons and opened up the door. He found, to his horror, the dead body of Archie Armstrong with a frightening look of terror and agony on his face. The air, ripe with the stench of his rotting corpse, caused those present to retch. It goes without saying that Sir Thomas was too late. It was thought, from the marks on Archie's body, that he had eaten his own forearm; cuts on his wrist suggested he tried to drink his own blood.

From that point on, Archie Armstrong not only haunted Haughton Castle, but Sir Thomas De Widdrington himself. Everywhere Sir Thomas went, he saw the pathetic ghost of Archie. It tormented him relentlessly for many months. Archie's ghost was said to have appeared at the dinner table, in what was normally an empty chair, and was seen to point menacingly at Sir Thomas. The ghost was also seen by Sir Thomas as he drifted off to sleep, and it was still there when he woke up in the mornings, grinning at him in the most maniacal of ways. He appeared on the stairwells of Haughton Castle and shrieked when Sir Thomas approached him.

Sir Thomas had had enough, and so an exorcist was brought in, from nearby Simonburn, to 'rid the castle of this pitiful spirit'. Using a blackletter Bible, this rite was successfully achieved. After the priest had done his work the angry spirit of Archie Armstrong was no more. Well, not until the Bible that was used for the exorcism was taken to London for major repairs in 1861. During the Bible's absence all hell broke loose, and the ghost of Archie Armstrong returned once more.

Subsequently, the return of the Bible was demanded immediately and once it was returned, the castle suffered no more psychic disturbances.

The good people of Barrasford do say, however, that the ghost of Archie Armstrong can still be seen, occasionally, when his ghost rises from out of the river and floats to the riverbank. Some say he has a bloodied arm raised over his head. It is also said that terrible wails and shrieks are often heard reverberating around the area of Barrasford. They are thought to have been gently carried there, on the wind. Another curious rumour suggests that screams can also be heard emanating from the castle itself, but only when descendants of Sir Thomas De Widdrington are in residence. One wonders if the old Bible is still locked away, deep inside Haughton Castle; the chances are it is. As a ghost hunter, I would the love to find out what would happen if this Bible were removed once again!

Hardriding farm, near Haltwhistle

In the middle of the fourteenth century, it is said that a well-known thief was murdered on Hardriding farm. No one knows why the robber was killed, but it's not hard to imagine. Perhaps the robber was to become the victim? If he had had a large amount of money on him, he would have been easy prey for other thieves. Perhaps he was burgling the farmhouse itself and disturbed the owners, resulting in a scuffle and a fight to the death? Maybe he was simply in the wrong place at the wrong time, and his death had nothing to do with his life of crime at all? No one knows for sure, although all these possibilities are certainly plausible.

Many years ago, in 1933, the inhabitants of the farm were woken from their slumber by the sound of a man shouting and their doors being perpetually opened and then slammed shut. Bemused, and rather frightened – to say the very least – they made their way to where the noises were seemingly coming from, only to find nothing occurring at all – neither inside or outside the farmhouse. This, of course, was much to their relief as they had thought that their home was being burgled. After a thorough search of the property they returned to their beds. So where were the noises coming from? Well, they put it down to the ghost of the murdered robber, making his annual visit to the area to mark his death. Local legend has it that this robber, makes his presence known every 100 years. Clive Kristen, a writer and authority on Northumbrian folklore, suggests that the last possible visit from the ghost marked 600 years since his murder. If so, that leaves only twenty-one years to wait (from the time of writing) to see if the phantom robber will make his presence felt again, in 2033. It's a long time to wait to verify a haunting.

Holystone Village

The village of Holystone lies on the edge of the Northumbria National Park, on the north side of the River Coquet. Labelled by the Northumberland National Park authorities as 'one of the most intriguing and enigmatic settlements', this wonderful old hamlet has an enchanting ecclesiastical and religious history. An Augustinian Priory for nuns was founded there, in the days of David I of Scotland. However, it was sadly one of the first religious buildings to be targeted by Henry VIII, at the onset of his Dissolution. Interestingly, nowadays a lot of this tiny little village is built upon the old site of this one-time nunnery. Remnants of the actual foundation stones can still be seen in various areas.

To the north of Holystone lies the famous 'Lady's Well', which, some say, has Roman origins. It is a popular visitor attraction in these parts. It is thought that the nuns of Holystone once tended this 'holy well', which produced pure-Northumbrian spring water; it can be seen to this day. The well is situated amongst a copse of trees and it is cared for by the National Trust. It is still, to this day, a wonderful and serene place to visit, should one want to 'become one with nature', or indeed, to simply contemplate the great mysteries.

Of course, with a religious history, the ghost enthusiast, or indeed the reader of this book, may expect to see or hear about spectral sisters of mercy frequenting the area … and you would be right. In fact, the pub in the village, called the Salmon Inn, was the scene of a 'ghostly nun'. One night, many years ago, a guest of the then owners woke to find her standing silently at the bottom of his bed. The pub, it seems, is built slap-bang in the middle of the former nunnery!

There are also reports of this silent phantom being seen at the bedside of sick people. On one occasion she was observed by the bedside of a severely ill man. Perhaps she was watching over him? On very rare occasions, the spectral nun has been spotted around the village at dusk, only to disappear into thin air, in the blink of an eye.

One wonders, out of all the nuns that once frequented this area, why this particular nun should 'come back', so to speak, and haunt the village. Or are my assumptions incorrect? Could it be that the numerous sightings of the ghost nuns at Holystone are in fact different spirits? After all, they would

An artist's impression of the ghost nun that was seen by the side of the bed of the then owners of the Salmon Inn, at Holystone Village. (Courtesy of Julie Olley)

have all been dressed the same, wouldn't they? One nun or a superfluity of nuns? It's a mystery to ponder over.

The local inn was also subject to other kinds of ghostly goings-on a few years back. A mischievous poltergeist-like entity played havoc with the owner's keys and other such belongings. On many occasions, the proprietors – John and Sylvia Gilbertson – found that their keys had been removed from their locks, only to find them back inside their keyholes weeks later. Footsteps were often heard to thump and bump up the stairwell of the pub, when no one else was inside the property. This phenomenon was put down to a phantom, said to be a Civil War Royalist, who had taken refuge in the old inn. He is said to have hidden inside one of the building's priest holes, where-upon the innkeeper, at that time, starved him to death. Apparently, it was too great

a risk for the landlord to keep feeding his walled-up guest, so he closed it up and left him to starve to death.

Clive Kristen nailed it in his book when he said the pub in Holystone should 'be awarded a special rosette by the good ghost guide as you will certainly get more than you bargain for if you order spirits in here'.

Knaresdale Hall, Near Haltwhistle

Knaresdale Hall stands to the south of Haltwhistle in Northumberland, and the ghost story attached to the place is a tragic one. It began when the middle-aged Laird of Knaresdale Hall was given permission to marry a beautiful young lady who was very wealthy. Unfortunately, the young girl in question did not want to marry the

Laird, but in those times, escaping arranged marriages was nigh on impossible. The girl, much to her dismay, married the Laird, but she never lived happily ever after. After a period of time, it seemed the girl began to settle down and became accustomed to her married life. However, it was all a charade. The girl had begun an illicit affair with the Laird's young nephew, and it was this 'fling' that saw her through the endless days of her monotony with her husband. Their passionate love affair went on for some time, until, one day, their game was up. The Laird's niece happened to come across them while they were in the midst of a passionate embrace. However, the niece promised to keep quiet about the affair because she loved her brother so much. But, paranoid as caught-out lovers are, they were petrified that the young niece would reveal their secret to her uncle, so a plot was hatched, by the two lovers, to kill her. This was the only way they thought they could ensure her silence.

One night, when a storm was raging, they decided that it would be the right time to murder her. During the night, the Laird's wife woke her husband complaining that she could not sleep, due to a door at the back of the house that was banging in the wind. She suggested that he send his niece to close it. Reluctant to do so, but wanting to please his wife, he woke up his niece and asked her to go and lock the door. This is where the story takes a sinister turn. As the young girl was locking the door, her brother leapt out and grabbed her. He dragged her to the nearby pond, which was overflowing with rain water, and threw her in. He then held her under the dark and murky waters until she drowned. Once she was dead, he weighed down the lifeless corpse and threw it into the middle of the pond, making sure she sank to the very bottom. She would never be found there – or so he thought.

Meanwhile, the Laird was becoming anxious because his precious niece had not returned. Convinced, by his evil wife, that she had indeed returned, and was in her bed, the Laird returned to his slumber. Later, he was woken from his sleep by the sound of his dogs howling. After sitting up in his bed, to see what was going on, he was surprised to see his beautiful niece standing in the room next to the roaring fire. She was dripping wet, caked in mud, and was ringing out the water from her long hair.

He got out from his bed and approached her, but she disappeared into thin air, in front of his eyes. He now began to suspect that his beloved niece was dead. His nephew was never seen again, and his wife went slowly insane, thinking about the part she played in the death of the young girl. After some time, as her dementia deepened, she began to unwittingly disclose information about the young girl's death through her insane rants. Most importantly, she let slip where her body was hidden. The Laird immediately had his pool dredged and was devastated to find the remains of his niece.

Not long after the discovery of the girl's body, the Laird's wife died. No one knows what happened to the Laird's young nephew, the perpetrator of the cruel deed. It is said that the ghost of the dead girl can be seen in and around the area of Knaresdale Hall on the anniversary of the tragic murder. She is, most often, seen walking from the back of the house to the pond where she was so brutally and cruelly murdered. At the same time, it is believed by some that the door that she tried to close, and lock, on the night of her death, springs open violently and swings on its hinges.

Longstone Lighthouse, Farne Islands

In researching this book I came across the tale of the Longstone Lighthouse ghost, whilst flicking through Sarah Hapgood's *500 British Ghosts and Hauntings*. I had never known that the Lighthouse was haunted by Grace Darling. However, before we go into the ghost of Grace, let us first remind ourselves of who Grace Darling was, and how she became a heroine in Northumbrian history.

Grace Horsley Darling was born on 24 November 1815. Her father William was the lighthouse keeper and so she spent much of life at Longstone. One terrible and stormy night, in 1838, Grace spotted a ship in distress out in the choppy and treacherous North Sea. The ship was called the SS *Forfarshire* and it was only a stone's throw from where Grace and her father were situated. People were hurling themselves from the doomed vessel into the ice-cold seas. The masts had broken and the sails were down, leaving the ship at the mercy of the ocean. Knowing that jagged rocks lay beneath the surface of the sea, and that soon the whole crew would be dead, Grace and her father launched their longboat and began a rescue attempt.

Despite knowing that they were risking their own lives, by rowing out to the distressed ship, they persevered with their mission nonetheless. The rescue was Borderline suicidal – however, neither Grace nor her father ever wavered in their attempt. The pair rowed out to sea over waves reaching 20ft in height and through gale-force winds of up to 100mph. Yet they rowed, and rowed, and continued to defy all the odds until they reached the crew of the *Forfarshire*. By this point, however, a lot of the ship's crew had already perished – but

Longstone Lighthouse on the Farne Islands off the Northumberland coast, said to be the home of the ghost of Grace Darling.

Grace Darling a year or two before her death. (Courtesy of the Newcastle Libraries and Information Service)

The Grace Darling memorial that stands proud in the graveyard of St. Aidan at Bamburgh.

it could have been the entire crew, had it not been for the brave efforts of one young lady and her father. Out of sixty-three people on the ship that night, nine were rescued – this was a night that these people would never forget. The survivors of the sinking ship, along with Grace and her father, returned to Longstone Lighthouse and stayed on the island for a further three days, until the weather was calm enough to return to the mainland port at Seahouses.

It is an incredible story of immense bravery, and is one of the north-east of England's most-celebrated historic events. However, only four years later, at the young age of twenty-six, Grace was to contract tuberculosis. She passed away on 4 October 1842. There is a wonderful

museum dedicated to her, and her selfless act of bravery, in nearby Bamburgh, and her memorial stands proudly in the graveyard of St Aidan just over the road from the museum.

Grace's ghost, it is said, stands atop the Longstone Lighthouse wearing a long brown dress and staring out to sea. One woman from Northumberland claims not only to have seen her, but to have photographed her too. While out on a boat trip around the Farne Islands, she claimed to have seen Grace at the top of the lighthouse. She took a picture but (as is usual in cases like this) the figure did not appear on the picture after it was developed. It was then that she realised that she must have seen the ghost of Grace Darling.

Sarah Hapgood tells the tale of two lighthouse keepers who claim to have heard unexplained footfalls 'clumping around' in the lighthouse's engine rooms; they suggest that it is Grace Darling in her clog boots. Interviewed on television, in 1976, the two lighthouse keepers were adamant the lighthouse was indeed haunted. However, in 1991, on a radio interview, the last-ever lighthouse keepers were interviewed and when asked if they thought the lighthouse was haunted they said, 'No'. It just goes to show that not everyone can experience ghostly phenomena in haunted locations.

Lord Crewe Arms, Blanchland

Possibly the most famous 'pub ghost' in the whole of the north east of England is that of Lady Dorothy Forster. She was the niece of both the Bishop of Durham and Lady Crewe respectively, and was sister to the famous Northumbrian general, Tom Forster, who was a leader of Jacobite Rebellion of 1715.

The Lord Crewe Arms, built in the twelfth century, was part of Blanchland Abbey, which was set in the beautiful and picturesque Derwent Valley, in the heart of the North Pennines. It is a former abbots' house, and is now classed as an ancient monument and a grade II listed, four-star inn.

The ghost of Dorothy Forster dates from the sixteenth century; she haunts the room in which she waited for her brother's return from the rebellion. Her sad, lonely ghost has been seen staring out of the window, in torment. Having been in the room for a look around, during a visit there in the late 1990s, I can say, in all sincerity, that the room did indeed have a certain 'feel' to it. I am not sure if this feeling was supernatural, or if it was to do with the ambience of the

entire establishment, as it is an atmospheric place to visit. At the time of my visit, on the wall outside the Bamburgh Suite (Dorothy's Room), was an old painting of Dorothy Forster. As I walked past, and looked at her, it felt as though she was looking straight back at me. It was if she knew I was there looking for her. Sadly, the only Dorothy I encountered on that day was, of course, the one in the painting. It may have been a different story for Rita Atkinson, however.

Without ever hearing about the ghosts of the Lord Crewe Arms, civil servant Rita, and her husband, Brian, booked into the hotel for a three-night stay, back in the early 1970s. On the first night of her stay, after spending a nice evening in the hotel bar downstairs, she retired to her room and locked the bedroom door. Soon both she and Brian drifted off into a nice sleep. During the night, however, she was suddenly awoken by the sound of footsteps outside her bedroom door. For a brief moment she lay there listening, until she heard her bedroom door open and then close with a click. The shuffling footsteps made their way across her bedroom floor, as she lay there terrified – all the while trying to wake her husband. The room temperature suddenly plummeted to almost freezing point, in which her breath could be clearly seen; at this point she was, in her own words, 'beside herself'. When I asked Rita if she experienced anything else, at that time, she quickly replied, 'Oh yes, I could feel something in the room with me, there was definitely someone there.' She went on to tell me that her husband slept through this strange occurrence. When she told her husband the following morning, he laughed it off and told her she was going mad. That was enough for Rita, though: that day she packed her bags and left the inn, after staying only one night of

A rear view of the Lord Crewe Inn at Blanchland.
Famously haunted by Lady Dorothy Forster – and
by one or two others, by all accounts.

The Lord Crewe Inn at Blanchland.

The Lord Crewe Inn in 1966. (Courtesy of the
Newcastle Libraries and Information Service)

her three-night reservation; she has never returned.

Brian eventually came round to the idea of ghosts many years later, when he was working in a shop in Devonshire Street, in Carlisle. One day he saw the figure of an old woman with grey hair making her way along the passageway inside the shop. There was no one else in the shop with him and the doors were locked. He followed the grey-haired lady down the corridor – where she disappeared. Bamboozled by this occurrence, he came to the conclusion that he had seen an apparition of some sort. This cast Rita's frightening experience of many years before at the Lord Crewe Arms in a new light. At last, he believed his wife's ghostly encounter.

Another ghost has been seen at the Lord Crewe Arms but this ghost is not discussed as often; Lady Dorothy always seems to overshadow it. Shame really, because this ghost has made its appearance far more recently! A couple who were spending the night in the Radcliffe Room – who were unaware that they were staying in a part of the hotel that was once frequented by monks known as 'the White Cannons' – woke up during the night to see a figure in white kneeling down at the foot of their bed. Feeling brave, the lady reached down with her hand and touched the figure of the white monk. She said that 'it felt solid'. After a few minutes, the figure slowly began to dissolve until she could no longer see it.

Lindisfarne, Holy Island

Perched high on a craggy rock, Lindisfarne Castle, on Holy Island, is a magnificent sight to behold. It was built around 1550 and was converted into a 'comfortable home' in the early 1900s, by Sir Edwin Lutyens. The castle, and the area in which it is situated, has to be one of the most sacred and holy places in the north of England. One never gets tired of visiting Holy Island – which has, for a long time, been known as the cradle of Christianity. I make the effort to get there at least two or three times every year. I remember the last time I visited Lindisfarne I walked the entire perimeter of the island on what was probably the worst day, for weather, that year. You see, for me, Holy Island is a place that can be enjoyed all year round. If you choose to visit, take time to study the causeway timetable, because there are very quick and rather dangerous in-coming tides … you don't want to get stranded, or worse.

St Aidan arrived at Lindisfarne in AD 664. He was a saint that was celebrated for his divine powers and also his amazing self-restraint. He was known as St Aidan of Lindisfarne, as he was the founder, and the first Bishop, of the monastery on the island – Lindisfarne Priory. A Christian missionary, St Aidan is most renowned for bringing Christianity back to Northumbria. He died in AD 651.

Thirteen years later, in AD 664, St Cuthbert (634-687) arrived on Holy Island. Cuthbert was elected the Bishop of Lindisfarne in AD 684, in a synod in a small seaside village of Twyford (it is now known as Alnmouth). Ironically, Alnmouth is home to one of the most haunted hotels in Britain, the Schooner.

Rather reluctant to leave his retirement and take up his new post, he was eventually persuaded to do so by King Ecgfrith of Northumbria. After being consecrated in York on 26 March 685, St Cuthbert returned to the Farne Islands, where he passed away on 20 March 687. After being taken to Lindisfarne for burial, his remains were eventually exhumed and transferred to the city of Durham.

The ghost of St Cuthbert is said to haunt this holy island. He has purportedly been seen sitting on the craggy rocks down by the shore. He also been seen inside the ruin of the old Priory, sitting on a stone slab. Legend has it that, on dark and stormy nights, he sits on the rocks shrouded in an eerie mist, chipping away at the stones. The sound of his light hammering as he works – tap, tap, tap – can be heard, as he makes what the locals refer to as 'Cuthbert Beads' or 'Cuddy's Beads'.

According to local legend, and folklore, it was said that St Cuthbert used the beads as a rosary, and that his earthbound spirit makes them so they could be found on the beach the following morning.

Sir Walter Scott, in his poem 'Marmion' (1808), describes St Cuthbert as he makes his beads:

> … Saint Cuthbert sits, and toils to frame
> The sea-born beads that bear his name:
> Such tales had Whitby's fishers told
> And said they might his shape behold,
> And here his anvil sound:
> A deadened clang – a huge dim form
> Seen but and heard when gathering storm
> And night were closing round.
> But this, a tale of idle fame,
> The nuns of Lindisfarne disclaim.

Lindisfarne is also home to a number of other ghosts; one, allegedly, is a Cromwellian soldier who has been seen at the castle. Peter Underwood, in his book, *This Haunted Isle*, states that Lindisfarne was a royalist garrison of Charles I that was besieged, and then taken by the Parliamentarians in 1644. He suggests – and quite rightly so – that 'this event may account for the reputed ghost',

The causeway at Lindisfarne, Holy Island.

a spirit that has been seen there on many occasions. A choir boy who resided on the island many years ago once told the Revd A. W. Jackson that he often saw the phantom of a monk, who disappeared through a wall. Described as a tall man, wearing a brown or black robe, and clasping a parchment, this monk was believed to have been St Cuthbert. Other monks have also been seen moving across the causeway, walking in procession. These monks, according to some people, were brutally murdered during the Viking raids of AD 793.

Elliot O'Donnell has written about Holy Island too. He says that a large-white hound haunts the priory ruins, and quite often startles people when it emerges

Lindisfarne Castle on Holy Island. Below the castle and sitting on the rocks (as well as inside the old priory), the ghost of St Cuthbert can be seen on stormy nights chipping away at the rocks, making his famous 'Cuddy's Beads'.

A statue of St Cuthbert on Holy Island with Lindisfarne Castle in the background.

from behind the stone walls and pillars. It is thought that this ghost dog runs towards the unsuspecting and frightened people that see it, before disappearing in a disturbing and most curious manner.

I will leave the final word, however, to Peter Underwood. When discussing the ghost of St Cuthbert in the aforementioned book, *This Haunted Isle*, he states that:

> Perhaps the most famous appearance of this ghost, if not the best authenticated, is the occasion when it was seen by Alfred the Great, who was a fugitive at the time. The ghostly saint indicated that all would be well and that Alfred would one day sit on the throne of England, and so it came to pass.

Oliver's Bar, Blyth

I first heard about the ghost of Oliver's Wine Bar after it was brought to my attention by a work colleague, Peter Hansen. Peter was born and bred in Blyth and so he is familiar with all its drinking houses and dens. The story of Oliver's Bar is a fascinating one. It begins when the bar was originally a butcher shop on Bridge Street in Blyth. It is believed that the butcher committed suicide by hanging himself from one of the hooks that was used to hang the carcasses from. No one knows why the butcher decided to end his life, but it's safe to say that he must have been pretty hacked off about something. A lost love? Money worries? Marital problems? We can only speculate.

After the butcher's shop closed down, a newsagents' shop was opened; but, by all accounts, no sightings of the ghost were ever reported. It was not until the pub opened, in December 1990, that people started seeing the ghostly figure. The figure of a man, wearing a long-brown butcher's apron, pass through the bar area before disappearing into thin air. The point at which the ghost vanishes happens to be the exact spot where the butcher hanged himself. It is said that many people have seen the spectral butcher inside the pub, and each time he does the same thing: he walks through the premises before vanishing.

The owner, Caroline, confirmed that the sightings began after the pub had opened in 1990, although, admittedly, she has never seen the ghost butcher herself. She did mention that, although it had been unusually quiet in the bar lately (referring to the ghost), the ghost often shows himself around the 27th of each month. Why around the 27th? Again, we can only guess. It does however make my job a bit easier when I go looking for him – which I will – soon!

She also let me in to some of the other ghostly phenomena which she has experienced during her tenancy of the pub. This

Oliver's Pub in Blyth is haunted by the ghost of a former butcher, who once worked on these very premises. Said to have hanged himself, his tormented soul still lingers around to this day. He is, however, only seen at night. (Courtesy of Mark Winter)

included interference with the beer kegs in the cellars – they were turned off to look as though they had failed! Light bulbs were often twisted out of their fittings and cold draughts, or 'spots', were often felt. Caroline then told me about the hairdresser's shop that is situated above the pub. They, too, have experienced ghostly activity, with things moving around on their own and inexplicable noises emanating from nowhere. The owners of the hairdressers claim that their paranormal activity stems from the haunting in the pub downstairs. You would think there would be no love lost in this case but both property owners are very friendly with one another. They take it all in their stride and are both rather fascinated by the shenanigans of the tragic butcher.

An artist's impression of the spectral butcher that has been seen inside of Oliver's Bar. (Courtesy of Julie Olley)

Otterburn Towers Hotel and Otterburn Battlefield

Built by William the Conqueror's cousin, Robert de Umfreville in 1086, Otterburn Towers – in Otterburn, Northumberland – is a remarkable antiquated and picturesque hotel.

The complex is set in 30 acres of lush countryside, with many woodland walks, and as much aesthetic beauty as one could wish for. Being situated in Otterburn, it is not hard for you to imagine that the Pele tower – for that is what it was originally – was subjected to many attacks from the Scottish invasions. You would, of course, be correct. In fact, on one occasion the Scots took Otterburn Tower, following the Battle of Otterburn. This was fiercest siege Otterburn Towers was ever subjected too. During the Battle of Otterburn (19 August 1388), the Earl of Douglas, and his men, faced the Percy army (which was led by Sir Henry 'Harry' Hotspur). It is said that over 10,000 men lost their lives on that fateful night, with the Scots emerging victorious. However, they suffered the loss of their leader, Douglas. Douglas was believed to have been killed – early on in the battle – by Harry Hotspur himself.

The land, soaked in the blood of both English and Scottish warriors, is now reputed to be haunted. It is said that the phantom armies have been seen, as they silently re-enact the gruesome battle that took place over 600 years ago. People have heard the sounds of galloping horses, growing louder and louder, as if they were coming towards them, only for them to gallop past – and into the distance – without an actual horse being seen. Battle cries and screams of pain are also rumoured to reverberate around the area, on occasions, with the accompanying, and unmistak-

Otterburn Towers Hotel in Otterburn. A spectacular edifice built by William the Conqueror's cousin Robert de Umfreville in 1086. It is haunted by a 'Grey Lady'.

able, sound of the clashing of steel on steel. Battered and bloody soldiers have also been seen, wandering aimlessly, as they cross the nearby roads and lanes.

Otterburn Tower is, of course, haunted too. Strange occurrences have been reported there for many years, with the sighting of a ghostly woman, who is thought to meander around the corridors at night. Simply known as 'the Grey Lady', no one knows who she really is. Other phenomena have been witnessed, late at night, in many of the bedrooms; strange smells that disappear as quickly as they come; whispering in rooms that are known to be empty, and harrowing screams are said to echo around the hotel.

An investigation was held there in 2004, by one of the north-east's original ghost hunting teams, and, by all accounts, a very interesting night was had. However, a week prior to the ghost-hunting team's vigil a strange incident was reported by some guests at the hotel: it appears that a window which had been bolted shut suddenly opened of its own accord; a couple were actually sitting next to it when it opened. In the excitement that ensued – as they stared, dumbfounded, at the window – the couple claim that their drinks were mysteriously swapped around on the table. Was this the work of the mysterious Grey Lady? Or does the hotel have a number of other denizens of the next world, just waiting to surprise you when you least expect it?

This site of the Battle of Otterburn, where the Earl of Douglas and his men faced the Percy army, led by Sir Henry 'Harry' Hotspur, on the 19 August 1388.

Situated in a small copse of trees close to the site of Otterburn's battle stands the Percy Cross, the commemorative stone marker a memorial to the dead.

The Percy Arms Hotel, Otterburn Village

Standing on the side of the Jedburgh Road, as you pass through the tiny village of Otterburn, is the Percy Arms Hotel. The hotel's website gives a beautiful description of the establishment, and its wondrous environs, by saying that, 'In the midst of a wild and romantic landscape, the Percy Arms Hotel stands on the edge of the Northumberland Moors'.

While driving one night – on a visit to the nearby Elsdon Gibbet, during a search for a petrol station – Mark Winter, and I, stumbled across the hotel in search of fuel.

We chatted to the staff and happened to ask if the hotel had any ghosts to which they replied, 'Yes, we do'. We were told about strange occurrences, which are often reported by guests, in particular bedrooms. However, they recommended that we speak to the owner, Clive Emerson, if we wanted to know more. This is exactly what I did. I returned to the hotel a month or two later and met up with him. I asked what he knew about the most active ghost that resides in the hotel, to which he replied, 'You know, it's odd really because our most famous ghost is the one we know the least about'. This is the ghost of a woman that had been seen on the roof of the hotel.

He explained it was 'common knowledge' that the Percy Arms was haunted and that this ghost was 'doing the rounds' when he bought the hotel, over twenty-three years before, in 1988. This is all he knew about the spectral tile-walker, apart from the fact she is known locally as the 'Grey Lady'. One wonders who she could have been and why on earth she would haunt a rooftop. Perhaps she threw herself from the roof and killed herself? Maybe she was working up there and simply fell? She may even not have taken a tumble from the roof in the first place!

Another ghost resides in room 2. It was a few years back, when a couple booked in to the room for a few nights. The first couple of nights were peaceful and enjoyable; however, their break was to become a little odd. During their last night at the hotel, the couple were awoken during the night by the distant sound of horse's hooves and a faint neighing. They got up and looked out of the bedroom window, thinking they would see the offending horse on the road outside, but saw nothing. They were just about to return to their beds when, suddenly, they both saw the horse at the same time. Not outside though, but inside their room! It appeared on one side of the room and galloped loudly to the other side of the room before disappearing into the wall. It went as quickly as it had appeared, returning the room back to its original silence. The couple were convinced that the horse looked tangible. The couple eventually managed to get back to sleep after their ghostly ordeal. The following morning, they relayed the story to Clive. They also mentioned that the horse was mounted by a fierce-looking soldier 'dressed in old-fashioned clothing', although they could not identify what period it was.

The thought occurs this may have had something to do with the Battle of Otterburn, which, of course, took place half a mile down the road back on the 19 August 1388. However, since the description of the man on the horse is rather vague, to say the least, we cannot be certain. I don't doubt, for one minute, that this ghost sighting occurred – or any of them, for that matter. Clive seems an honest and reliable source of information, who, incidentally, told me all the ghost stories before he knew I was an author on the paranormal.

The Percy Arms Hotel in Otterburn. The author discovered a wealth of ghost tales and phantom encounters at this hotel, during numerous visits there. His investigations continue to this day.

In room 10, as recently as March 2010, the ghost of a woman was seen by a lady that had booked in with her family. The kids had been sleeping on zed-beds, and it was next to the children where the ghost woman was seen. The lady in question, woke up during the night feeling freezing cold, even though the heating system was on full. She sat up in her bed and then noticed a woman, dressed in a long gown, bending over her children and tending to the bedclothes. 'It was as though she was tucking the children in and keeping them warm,' Clive told me. She then stood upright, turned her back on the lady in the bed, and walked straight through the wall. The room's temperature returned to normal soon after.

Clive has also experienced water-related incidents at the hotel; he calls it 'the water mystery'. When I asked what he meant, he told me that he often finds damp patches in the walls where there is no damp present. Later on, these damp or wet patches are completely gone and no cause can be found for them. Pools of water often appear in the downstairs areas of the building, but no leaks have ever been found; often he has had to turn off taps that are forever being 'turned on'.

His final tale (but his first experience) goes back to 1988 when he and his family were celebrating Christmas. Sadly, during this particular festive season, his visiting father was taken ill and passed away on the 3 January. One year later – on 3 January

– the family were again at the hotel celebrating Christmas when the conversation turned to his beloved dad. They began to reminisce about the old times and subsequently began discussing the sad day he passed – one year ago to the day. Suddenly, the family were struck silent as a large plate mounted on the wall split in half with a huge 'crack'! Clive is 100 per cent certain that his dad was looking down upon them, watching them as they celebrated Christmas. 'It was perfect timing … just as we were discussing dad, that plate went! It was as though he was saying "hello son, I am here with you all, Merry Christmas".'

An artist's impression the ghost lady that was seen in room 10 at the Percy Arms Hotel, in 2010. (Courtesy of Julie Olley)

Schooner Hotel, Alnmouth

What self-respecting ghost hunter would write a book on Northumbrian ghosts, and leave out the most-haunted hotel that this county has ever seen? Not me, that's for sure! I quite often hear people talk of the Schooner Hotel and say things like, 'It's all a load of rubbish', or, 'I have stayed a night there and nothing happened, therefore its all baloney'. I guess the Schooner management advertising the fact that there are sixty ghosts (yes, you read that correctly – sixty) residing at this 400-year-old former coaching inn doesn't help the situation either. But let me tell you this: the Schooner Hotel is haunted. I have investigated the property on almost twenty occasions and had some of the most terrifying experiences I have had as a ghost hunter there.

Of course, I can imagine some sarcastic people saying, 'Well, if Darren said it's haunted it must be, mustn't it?' But don't take my word for it; do some research, find out what really goes on behind these ancient doors, or, better still, book a room! (Room 7 or 28 will do just nicely.)

For real eerie thrills and spills you need patience, and lots of it. But if anywhere can deliver a genuinely spooky experience, it will be the Schooner. The hotel is located in Alnmouth, on the Northumberland coast, which is just a few miles east of Alnwick. This hotel is a warren of corridors and rooms, and has been voted 'the most haunted hotel in the UK' on a number of occasions. Built around the seventeenth century, this magnificent edifice has become so well-known for its ghosts that there is not a weekend that goes by without it being investigated (sometimes by professionals, but mostly by weekend hobbyists and thrill seekers). With so many tales of suicide, murder, lost loves, tragedies,

Britain's most haunted hotel (reputedly): the Schooner in Alnmouth.

lies, deceit and smugglers, it is no wonder the Schooner Hotel claims to have so many resident ghosts.

Where do I begin? Let me start in the corridor next to room 20. Many years ago, a cleaner and another member of staff – the hotel secretary, I believe – was in the area carrying out some duties. As they approached the top of the stairwell, which leads to the long corridor, they were both horrified to see a large, black figure come running out of room 20. It then smashed headlong into the fire door that stood opposite. As the fire door failed to open, the large black shape had no where to go, so it turned, faced the two girls, and then began to run towards them, in the most peculiar way. They both turned and ran in an instant, fighting with one another to get down the flight of stairs first. I had the opportunity to speak to one of these witnesses, Corrina, who told me that this was one of the most frightening experiences she had ever had. She said there were no discernible features on this 'black shape' and when she returned soon after, with support, no one was to be found. 'It must have been a ghost,' she told me, 'and by God I do not want to run into that one again!'

Another of the Schooner's ghosts is known simply as 'William'. This chap was reputed to have butchered his family over 200 years ago, and yet he still walks the corridors and rooms 28, 29 and 30. This area of the hotel is the oldest section, and I have spent many an hour there searching for this William fellow. On one of my first ever investigations there, myself and a number of witnesses heard footsteps coming from the narrow corridor next to room 28. The floor boards were creaking and groaning, as though there was somebody outside the room, but a quick inspection found no one there; well, no one that we could see. I say that because when a co-investigator walked out into the corridor, he was halted in his tracks by someone standing in front of him. Someone was there, only we couldn't see him.

A ghost airman, who has been seen in full uniform, is said to walk the corridors by rooms 15-19. An old woman, with a walking stick, is also said to have been heard in the same area; the sound of her stick, tap, tap, tap tapping along the floor as she walks, has woken many guests staying in the nearby rooms. When they look out into the corridor, they find nobody.

The ghost of a young girl is said to haunt the area known as 'the Chase Bar'. The girl died on Christmas Day, 1802, after her mother accidentally dropped her onto a raging fire – she hit her head on the hearth in the process. This ghost girl meanders occasionally around the bar area. On one occasion, a visitor to the hotel heard the sound of a young girl laughing, coming from the bar area, but upon inspection found no one. Another lady said she saw a young girl come running round the corner: she stopped dead, looked at the woman, and then disappeared into thin air. The list goes on and on. With all the accounts that I have in my archives at home, one could write a book on the ghosts of the Schooner Hotel alone. However, I may save that task for another day.

I leave the reader with one of my own experiences at the Schooner Hotel which left me, and a friend of mine – Suzanne – very shaken up. We had been given the keys to the premises in the winter season and had full access to all areas. No guests were booked in and all the hotel staff had been given some time off. There was only myself and Suzanne in the building, so we wasted no time in getting on with the investigations. We began our investigations downstairs. While walking along the corridor, on the ground floor, we both thought we heard some noises coming from what was then called 'the Malcolm Miller' restaurant area. We looked at each other with nervous faces but decided we needed to venture inside the restaurant area.

I went first and slowly crept in, followed closely by Suzanne. As I entered the room, Suzanne began to take a few steps into the room, so at that point I closed the door. I pushed the door hard into the frame and distinctly heard the door 'click' into a locked position – Suzanne heard the door shut too. We stood there in silence and

An artist's impression the ghost lady with her walking stick that is said to haunt the corridors of the Schooner hotel. (Courtesy of Julie Olley)

listened out for the noises we had recently heard – but there was nothing. I then turned around and gasped at what I saw. This 'gasp' of air caught Suzanne's attention so she turned around to see what was going on. At that point we both watched the door – the door I had just moments ago closed with a click – opening very slowly and in a controlled manner. The door opened almost all of the way before coming to rest for a brief second or so. Suddenly, and with no one near it, it slammed closed with such speed and force that the noise it made almost brought the ceiling down on our heads. To put it mildly, we almost passed out with fright.

This happening, as well as many other frightening experiences – detailed in many of my other books – are my personal testimonies; they support my belief that the Schooner Hotel is a very haunted building. I don't care what other people say, and I don't give a damn if they don't believe me: the fact is, this happened.

Silky's Bridge, Black Heddon

If you drive up the A696 – otherwise known as the Newcastle to Jedburgh Road – you will reach the tiny village of Belsay. About half a mile after Belsay you will reach a turn off (B6309), which takes you to Stamfordham Village, where the aforementioned Bay Horse Public house is. However, it is not the Bay Horse Pub we wish to visit on this occasion, but a small village called Black Heddon. Black Heddon lies about half way down the B6309 and is a village with a terrifying spectre. An old stone hump-back bridge once stood here but it has subsequently been replaced by another. This old bridge was simply known as Silky's Bridge.

Silky's Bridge was christened thus over 200 years ago, by locals, after a so-called witch lived beneath it. She wore a black silk dress and was said to have resided in an old shack just down by the riverbank. Some people suggest that this woman, in black, was no more a witch than the next person, but more of a cunning and manipulative thief, who wore black and robbed the locals of their hard-earned money. Regardless of who she really was, legend says that she was trampled to death by a number of villagers with their horses. They had had enough of her evil thieving ways, although they had only intended to frighten her away and not actually kill her.

After her death, the spectre of this woman, dressed in black, was seen at the spot where she died; the spot was the approach to the old bridge. The ghost was often said to scare the living daylights out of the horses that used the roads, resulting in them shying up, on their two hind legs, before bolting off into the distance. Other times the horses were so frightened by the sound of her 'rustling dress' that they froze solid and refused to venture any further forward, much to the annoyance of those

Black Heddon, between Belsay and Stamfordham.

The road into Black Heddon, where the ghost of a witch has been seen standing by the side of the road. This was once an accident black spot for which the ghost was blamed.

people with them. Quite often she is seen standing in the middle of the road, her eerie, chilling presence stopping people in their tracks, forcing them to head back from whence they came and to find a new route to their final destination.

Nowadays Silky is not heard of much, nor is she seen that often, but reports do occasionally come in regarding strange things that occur in the spot that leads to the now-modern bridge. People who pass that way sometimes feel they are not alone, and quite often get the sensation of being 'followed home'. Could this be Silky? Other people have been driving past in their cars when, suddenly, their engine cuts out for no reason whatsoever ... could this be Silky? Who knows? I drove past this very spot on the way to Stamfordham in May 2010, during the course of my research for this book, and made it past this area in question – twice – with no trouble whatsoever. However, when I stopped to take pictures I left my engine running... just in case it didn't start again!

I will finish with a quote from Jack Hallum, author of *Ghosts of the North*:

A figure in glistening and rustling silk, moving like a sudden gust of wind in the trees – that is Silky – the ghost of Black Heddon Bridge.

Thirlwall Castle and the Ghostly Guardian Dwarf

Thirlwall Castle, like many old buildings from a bygone age – where sieges were rife and death was in abundance – lies derelict, worn, and in a ruined state. Sadly, very little of it remains. It is located just outside of the boundary of Northumberland National Park, just 3 or 4 miles north of Greenhead. The castle lies close to where Hadrian's Wall once stood – and still does in some respects – and was said to have been built by some of the stones from a nearby Roman fort.

The castle was originally built in the 1200s but was modified and strengthened by John Thirlwall in the mid-1330s. The Thirlwalls were a very wealthy family and had made copious amounts of money over the years so they could easily afford the renovation work that the castle so badly needed. Of course, being a clued-up individual, John Thirlwall, was fully aware of the fact that his home would be at risk from Border Wars, raids from the Scots, and rogue bandits etc, so he decided to turn his house into a fortified bastion. Doing this he kept himself, his family and, most importantly, his fortunes safe.

This seems to have done the trick, as no one managed to take his castle. A fellow author and close friend, Rob Kirkup, tells us in his commendable book, *Ghostly Northumberland*, that 'several generations of Thirlwalls survived the threat of Border raids' with the castle still being in the hands of the Thirlwall family in 1542. By the 1700s the Thirlwalls had moved on from their home of 300 years, and had relocated to Hexham. The castle and grounds were bought by the Earl of Carlisle in 1748 but according to Kirkup, 'he was only interested in the value of the land and allowed the castle to become overgrown and decay until it became a derelict shell'.

Preserved by the National Park Authorities in 1999, the remains of Thirlwall Castle were 'made safe' for tourists and visitors.

Legend has it that there is a tunnel – dating back to the time of the wars between the English and the Scots – that leads from Thirlwall Castle to nearby Blenkinsopp Castle, in which a 'White Lady' walks. However, this account relates more to Blenkinsopp Castle than it does Thirlwall, as the reader will recall after reading the Blenkinsopp Castle section of this book.

Moving on then … there is another ghost tale connected to Thirlwall Castle. It is a story that, I feel, definitely belongs in the realms of folklore and involves a hideous dwarf that guards the treasure of John Thirlwall. It is said that during one of his many trips away he brought back a table made of solid gold. The table's guardian was said to have been this ugly-looking, dark-skinned dwarf. So, with his treasures safety in mind, John brought the dwarf back with him too. During a subsequent raid from the Scots, the dwarf dragged the solid-gold table through the castle and threw it down a deep well, to prevent it from being stolen by the Scottish invaders. However, not wanting to abandon his duties, he followed the table down and is said to be standing guard to this day.

Being unaware of his dwarf's plans to protect the table, John Thirlwall thought his 'now missing' table had been stolen by the raiders. He spent the rest of life trying to track it down, but to no avail; he died a very unhappy man. If, by chance, you, the reader, are an only son of a widow, then I suggest you get yourself to Thirlwall Castle. I say this because legend has it that the only

Thirlwall Castle is a peculiar old ruin. The ghost of a dwarf is alleged to watch over some hidden treasure that is buried deep underground, under the ruin. (Courtesy of the Newcastle Libraries and Information Service)

person that the dwarf will give up the table for is the only son of a widow. I suggest you get yourself to Thirlwall Castle, find the underground chamber, in which the table and its guardian sits, and collect your reward. By the way, if you go and meet this ugly little creature, do let me know ... oh, and send me a picture of it.

John Thirlwall's search for his long-lost treasure goes on in death, as it did in life, it seems. It is said that, on moonlit nights, his restless shade can be observed as it flits from one place to the next, looking endlessly for his lost table.

A colleague of mine (and someone that you, the reader, will now be familiar with), John Triplow has spent much of his spare time investigating many of the alleged haunted sites in Northumberland; Thirlwall Castle being one of his favourite places. I asked him about his research into the alleged hauntings that have occurred in the ruins; he was happy to share his thoughts with me:

In late 2008, I was contacted by a good friend, and colleague, of mine, Gail Ward, who initially brought the old-Thirlwall ruin to my attention. According to what I had been told by Gail, the castle was reputedly haunted and the stories connected to it had helped form an integral part of Haltwhistle's historic folklore. Intrigued, I decided to contact the owners of the property in the hope that they would grant us permission to conduct an investigation at the ruin: fortunately they agreed.

The following February my partner, Kelly, and I, arranged to meet with Gail at her home before heading over to Thirlwall Castle. If my memory serves me right, the weather conditions that night were less than fantastic. In fact, the whole country had been hit by an abhorrent snowfall that preceding week, and it was still bitterly cold. Undeterred, we cracked on with the job regardless.

Throughout the course of the night, Gail mentioned that she was being constantly distracted by what sounded like 'a female singing'. I tried to hear what Gail had described but my gut instinct was that she was hearing a combination of the nearby Tipalt Burn, which runs rapidly by one side of the castle, integrating with other background sounds, which were causing an illusion that almost sounded like the faint echoing of a female voice.

At about 3 a.m. it was unbearably cold, so we decided to draw the investigation to a close. Kelly, Gail and I hiked down the side of the hill towards a gravel path that would eventually lead us back to the car. We had only walked about 20 metres or so along the path before the three of us stopped dead in our tracks. Open mouthed, we glared at each other and simultaneously blurted out, 'What the hell was that...?' We had all heard a loud, distinctly female voice boom from within the castle – and 'she' was singing! Luckily, I had left my recorder running during that time and successfully managed to capture the strange, ethereal voice.

But what interested me more than anything was the discovery I made when I reviewed the recording: it was apparent that it had happened twice, although, it had only been audible once, when we were there. In retrospect, I am honoured to have experienced what I did. I only hope that one day (or night) I will encounter something of a similar nature again; the whole experience was indeed very touching.

Warkworth Castle, Warkworth

The keep at Warkworth castle is, probably, one of the best preserved keeps in the whole of the United Kingdom – and if you saw it from inside, you would agree. The castle, which is almost looped by the River Coquet, sits magnificently on a large hillock and, like Bamburgh Castle, completely dominates the entire area. Warkworth Castle lies around twenty-five miles down the Northumbrian coast from Bamburgh and is one mile, or so, from the small fishing village of Amble.

It was originally built by Henry, the Earl of Northumberland – who was the son of David I of Scotland – in the mid-twelfth century, as a motte and bailey construction. Warkworth Castle was yet another of the best-placed bastions in the area. Perched high on its hill, and surrounded by water, the only way in was from the south. It could not have been built on a better spot and it was a very well-defended castle.

In the thirteenth century the motte and bailey construction was replaced with stone. The castle eventually fell into the hands of the Lord of Alnwick, Henry De Percy, who carried out extensive work on the fortress, turning it into one of the best castles in the land. Over the years though, following many sieges and attacks on the castle, it fell into a semi-ruinous state. However, it then passed into the ownership of the Crown. After the castle was rebuilt, it was given back to the Percy family, who then forfeited its ownership once again. By 1470, however, it was back in the Percy's hands. Finally, in 1572, the castle was besieged and ruined one last time. However, this time it was not rebuilt as a home. In the mid-1600s the castle sustained further damage, when Parliamentary forces used the castle as a shelter. By the seventeenth century, local

Warkworth Castle has one of the best preserved keeps in the country and is undoubtedly one of the finest castles in Northumberland. It is haunted, however, by a man that thinks he is a dog!

people and other people, such as builders, were coming to Warkworth to make use of the ruins, taking the stones and bricks.

For a few hundred years, Warkworth Castle remained a battered and wind-swept ruin, until the 3rd Duke of Northumberland made the wise decision to carry out some preservation and restoration work. Some sections were rebuilt, while others were dug up and excavated. Now run by English Heritage, the castle is one of the north-east's most-popular visitor attractions.

That was the history: now for the mystery. The castle is alive with the dead; with so much bloody history attached to the castle, it's not hard to imagine that ghosts of individuals – long since dead – still flit about the ruins and in the dark depths of the keep. Like many other castles and historic fortresses, Warkworth Castle is alleged to have its fair share of spectres, and there any many reliable accounts to back up these claims.

Our first ghost is probably the most interesting account of a haunting we have from Warkworth Castle. It occurred on an autumnal afternoon back in the early 1970s. A school teacher, who was visiting the castle with pupils from her school, was surprised to see a man in the grounds who was dressed in old-fashioned attire and looked rather like an old soldier. She approached the man and commented upon how authentic he looked, and that it was nice that staff members had dressed up for the school's visit. The soldier was said to have looked confused. He said nothing to the lady, but turned around and walked into the keep. She followed him inside the castle, whereupon she saw the man take a left turn and then make his way up a flight of stone stairs. She followed him to the top of the stairs and turned the corner but she was surprised to see that that chamber led nowhere, as it was blocked off. There was only one way in and one way out – and yet the soldier was gone. Where did this man go? Who was he? And what had she just witnessed? When she asked the castle staff about a man dressed up they knew nothing of him. This, combined with the fact he just vanished into thin air, led her to believe she had seen a ghost. Had it not been for the fact that pupils also saw the soldier, before he ventured into the keep, she would have thought she imagined the whole thing.

Another ghostly encounter occurred when an evening stroller was meandering past the castle. Suddenly, she heard the clash of steel on steel accompanied by the thundering of horses' hooves. The roar of an army of men reverberated around the area, so, naturally, she thought there was an event going on inside the castle. She walked around to the front of the castle but, much to her surprise, she found the castle gates locked and no one else around. Peering inside the castle gates she could clearly see that the castle was closed and deserted. This bemused her somewhat as, by then, the sounds that she heard had ceased. When I spoke to this woman, who was, by sheer chance, on a trip to Warkworth one day, in 1994, I asked her what she thought it could have been. 'Undeniably the sounds of ghosts,' she told me. 'What else could it be?'

Another ghost of Warkworth is said to be that of a 'Grey Lady'. She has been seen floating around inside the keep, making her way from room to room, as if she is looking for something. According to Clive Kristen, in his amazing book, *Ghost Trails of Northumbria*, these ghost reports are 'rather unsatisfactory'. However, Rob Kirkup suggests in *Ghostly Northumberland* that this elusive 'Grey Lady' has been sighted on many occasions, with the swish of her dress being heard as she glides past. Rob even supplies an identity for her and suggests she is Lady Eleanor Neville, the wife of the 2nd Earl of Northumberland. Fascinating stuff.

By far the most famous ghost to reside at Warkworth castle is that of one Tom Sherratt (some say Tom Skerratt). Tom was held wholly responsible for the murder of Henry Percy, the 4th Earl of Northumberland, on 28 April 1489. However, he only played a minor part in his demise. He was arrested and placed in the dungeons at Warkworth Castle, whereupon the 5th Earl of Northumberland (another Henry Percy), would decide his fate. It took over two years for the 5th Earl to arrive at Warkworth and by then, through his imprisonment, Tom Sherratt had gone insane. The Earl was said to have taken great pity on him and, rather than have him killed, he was left in the care of the man who looked after the castle's hounds. From that point on he lived his life like a dog. He ran around on all-fours with the rest of pack and howled for his food whenever he became hungry.

Tom Sherratt actually outlived the 5th Earl by a matter of months and after his death he was buried in what was then known as 'the common pit'. This was where the curse of Tom Sherratt began, for his ghost was said to have come back and haunted the 6th Earl (yet another Henry Percy), with a vengeance. The 6th Earl of Northumberland remained childless and blamed the fact on Tom Sherratt's ghost. Had his father not treated him so badly, he may have been able to have had the children he so desired. Other Percy family members suffered untimely deaths, massive misfortunes, and incomprehensible defeats in battle; they too believed they were the victim of the Tom Sherratt's curse.

Nothing went right for the Percys after Tom Sherratt's death. Tom is still believed to haunt Warkworth Castle to this day. His chilling dog-like howls are still heard from time to time, as they reverberate around the giant keep. It seems, even in death, Tom Sherratt is insane and still believes he is a hound. A rather sad and tragic end, don't you think?

Woodhorn Colliery

Woodhorn Colliery on the outskirts of Ashington – like many other collieries – was sadly closed for business back in the early 1980s. Woodhorn Colliery was originally opened in 1894 and was a working coal mine for eighty years, before closing its doors back in 1981. Like other sites of this nature, the original buildings, which were once used during the pit's hey-days, were kept and eventually utilised as part of the colliery museum. Today, Woodhorn Colliery is acknowledged as one of the finest surviving examples of a working pit. This particular pit was actually the third colliery to be sunk, by the coal company in Ashington, with work commencing on the 16 May 1894 and finishing in 1898. A second shaft was added to the existing site soon after and, in 1901, it began to mine its first coal.

During its prime, Woodhorn Colliery employed almost 2,000 men, who, in turn, mined over six 600,000 tons of coal each year. By the late 1970s, however, production at Woodhorn had declined massively, leaving only 500 workers employed there. Today, this one-time coal mine is a museum that is dedicated to the history of coal mining, and is a wonderful place to go and visit. The buildings are, in actual fact, listed and are also classed as a scheduled monument.

Woodhorn Colliery near Ashington is the site of an amazing ghost tale.

For some reason, on which we can only speculate, mines and pits that produce commodities, such as lead and coal, are quite often associated with ghosts; perhaps due to the frequent explosions and other disasters that these types of mine were known to suffer from. Examples of haunted mines include Killhope Lead Mine, the old Springwell Colliery that now houses the Bowes Railway Museum, and, of course, Woodhorn Colliery.

There are many fascinating ghost tales associated with Woodhorn Colliery, the most famous being the unmistakable sounds of crying women. Many times these ladies have been heard, as the gentle weeping noise drifts across the mine and reverberates around, with no natural source ever being found for it. It is thought that the sound of crying women are an echo of

an event that quite often took place in the early days of the mining. Whenever a disaster should befall the hard-working miners – which was all too frequently – it is said that the wives of the workers would come from their nearby houses and gather at the pit gates, all the while crying in anguish; in the desperate hope of hearing good news regarding their men. Quite often, for many of the women and their families, the news was tragic and therefore the weeping went from a pitiful sob to an outright wail.

A wonderful tale, which is also well known, is the amazing account of the ghost that saved the lives of a group of men. They were crossing a walkway together one night when a young pit boss turned up, out of the blue, and turned them back. He told the men that it was 'unsafe' to venture forwards, so they turned round and headed back to where they had come from. Moments later a gas explosion rocked the empty gallery area, and brought down everything in it. Had the workers been there, they would have been killed. After the explosion the group of men went in search of the pit boss, to say 'thank you' to him for saving their lives, but could find no trace of him anywhere. Imagine their surprise when they discovered an old newspaper clipping with an article detailing the news of a similar gas explosion that occurred twenty-five years previously at the colliery. This explosion brought down the gallery and killed a man. The photograph of the dead man was featured in the newspaper, and it was that of the 'pit boss' who had turned the workers back minutes before the explosion that would have been killed them!

Yet another account of spectres at Woodhorn concerns a night-watchman who chased what he thought were intruders across a yard. These intruders were said to have been dressed as miners, but he challenged them nonetheless, as they should not have been there at that time. His suspicions were further aroused when the two men ran off. He gave chase, but eventually the night-watchman had to give up, as the two intruders ran straight into a brick wall and vanished! Rumours persist that the night-watchman was drunk, however, and had already downed a considerable amount of whiskey. Although whiskey is not hallucinogenic, it would be wise to treat this ghost sighting as 'unlikely', but let us not dismiss it entirely.

Another ghost comes in the shape of a phantom miner, who has been seen sobbing into has hands, with face and head blackened with coal; he disappears when people approach him. Woodhorn Colliery really is an amazing place, which is awash with spectral shades and echoes of the past. Researching this book has taught me this,

and I had a wonderful time visiting the area. I had planned on seeing one of the many residents ghosts, or maybe even hearing them, but alas, it was not to be … oh well, maybe next time?

Ye Olde Cross Pub, Alnwick

Tucked away on Alnwick's Narrowgate stands the pub nicknamed 'the dirty bottles'. It's name derives from the window display, of old and dusty bottles, that has been there for as long as anyone can remember. The pubs real name is Ye Olde Cross and it is, in my opinion, one of the finest little pubs Northumbria has to offer. The owners and staff are kind, they sell good beers and ales, and it is home to one of Northumberland's most terrifying curses. There is no pub in the land with such a fine legend as Alnwick's 'cursed bottles', and with its eerie and macabre prophecy of a supernatural and certain death, I dare say the bottle display will be there for many years to come.

Over 200 years ago, it is said that the owner of the property was preparing a window display when, suddenly, he suffered a fatal heart attack and dropped-down dead on the spot. The bottle display was, for some unknown reason, closed up in the window and left exactly how it was when the owner died. The legend suggests that if anyone touches the bottles inside the window display they too will suffer the fate of the original owner, and die instantly. I will tie up the dirty bottles section with a paragraph that I used in my book, *Supernatural North*. The paragraph sums up my thoughts quite nicely in regards to cynicism, and people's attitudes towards the paranormal. It reads:

> It's amazing to think that at one time the belief in such 'supernatural matters' were

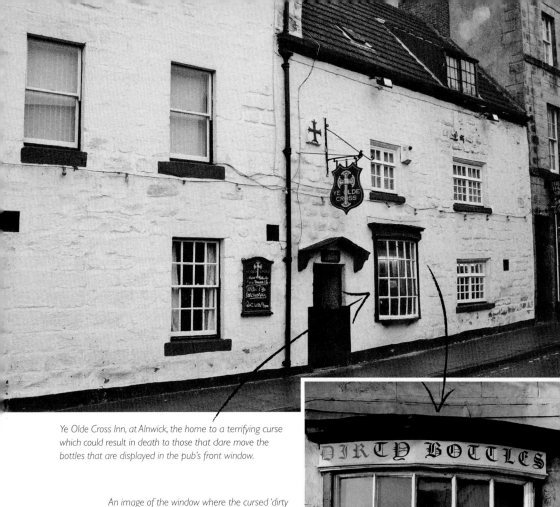

Ye Olde Cross Inn, at Alnwick, the home to a terrifying curse which could result in death to those that dare move the bottles that are displayed in the pub's front window.

An image of the window where the cursed 'dirty bottles' stand. Taken **c.** 1970. (Courtesy of the Newcastle Libraries and Information Service)

looked upon with scorn and ridicule, indeed ghosts and poltergeists are still widely rejected by the scientific community et al. Yet, over two hundred years have gone by since the window was locked up and no one to this day has dared to move the bottles … I think that tells us quite a lot about what people really think in regards to curses and old wives' tales, with the lack of actions in this case, speaking louder than the words!

Bibliography and Recommended Reading

Adams, P., Brazil, E. & Underwood, P., *The Borley Rectory Companion* (The History Press, 2009)

Coxe, Hippisley, A.D, *Haunted Britain* (Pan Macmillan, 1973)

Dodds, D., *Northumbria at War* (Pen and Sword, 2005)

Dodds, Lyndon G., *Historic Sites of Northumberland and Newcastle upon Tyne* (Albion Press, 2002)

Haining, P., *Ghosts: The Illustrated History* (BCA, 1974)

Hallowell, M.J. & Ritson, D.W., *The South Shields Poltergeist* (The History Press, 2008)

Hallowell, M.J. & Ritson, D.W., *The Haunting of Willington Mill* (The History Press, 2011)

Hallowell, M.J., *Christmas Ghost Stories* (Amberley, 2009)

Hallowell, M.J., *Mystery Animals of the British Isles – Northumberland and Tyneside* (CFZ Press, 2008).

Hallum, J., *Ghosts of the North* (David & Charles, 1976)

Hapgood, S., *500 British Ghosts and Hauntings* (Foulsham, 1993)

Harries, J., *The Ghost Hunter's Road Book* (Charles Letts & Co., 1968)

Kirkup, R., *Ghostly Northumberland* (The History Press, 2008)

Kirkup, R., *Ghostly Tyne and Wear* (The History Press, 2009)

Kirkup, R., *Ghostly County Durham* (The History Press, 2010)

Kristen, C., *Ghost Trails of Northumbria* (Casdec, 1992)

Matthews, R., *Mysterious Northumberland* (Breedon Books, 2009)

Puttick, B., *Supernatural England* (Countryside Books, 2002)

Ritson, D.W, *Ghost Hunter, True Life Encounters from the North East* (GHP, 2006)

Ritson, D.W, *In Search of Ghosts, Real Hauntings from Around Britain* (Amberley, 2008)

Ritson, D.W, *Haunted Newcastle* (The History Press, 2009)

Ritson, D.W, *Haunted Durham* (The History Press, 2010)

Ritson, D.W, *Haunted Berwick* (The History Press, 2010)

Ritson, D.W, *Ghosts at Christmas* (The History Press, 2010)

Ritson, D.W &, Hallowell, M.J, *Ghost Taverns* (Amberley, 2009)

Underwood, P., *A Gazetteer or British Ghosts* (Souvenir Press, 1971)

Underwood, P., *A-Z of British Ghosts* (Souvenir Press, 1971)

Other local titles published by The History Press

Haunted Berwick

DARREN W. RITSON

Here is a terrifying collection of true-life tales from around Berwick.
Take a tour of this ancient town from Berwick Castle to the town walls
and discover an unnerving assortment of poltergeists, spectres and myths,
including a witch's curse, the warning toll of a ghostly bell, chilling
vampiric encounters, and the inauspicious spirit of a weeping boy.

978 0 7524 5548 8

Haunted Durham

DARREN W. RITSON

From Durham Castle to Jimmy Allen's public house, discover poltergeists,
hooded apparitions, headless horses, phantoms, séances and exposed
hoaxes. Containing many tales which have never before been published –
including the crooked spectre of North Bailey and the ghost who bruised
a barmaid's backside – this book will delight everyone interested in the
paranormal.

978 0 7524 5410 8

The South Shields Poltergeist

MICHAEL J. HALLOWELL AND DARREN RITSON

Meticulously documented, *The South Shields Poltergeist* is a truly terrifying
account of the authors' struggle with an invisible, malicious entity. Their
encounter may well go down in the annals of psychical research as one of
the most chilling true-life encounters of its kind. From spectral assaults to
flying objects, phone calls from beyond the grave and children's toys that
spoke to the investigators it will thrill readers everywhere.

978 0 7524 5274 6

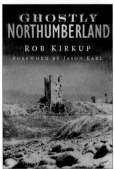

Ghostly Northumberland

ROB KIRKUP

Ghostly Northumberland investigates twenty of the most haunted locations
in Northumberland today. This selection includes a piano-playing ghost
at Bamburgh Castle, the White Lady of Cresswell Tower, a mischievous
poltergeist at the Schooner Hotel, as well as sightings of torturer Jogn Sage,
who continues to stalk the dungeons at Chillingham Castle. Illustrated
with over fifty photographs, together with access details for each location,
this book is sure to appeal.

978 0 7509 5043 5

If you are interested in purchasing other books published by The History Press, or in case you have difficulty
finding any of our books in your local bookshop, you can also place orders directly through our website
www.thehistorypress.co.uk